CLOSING
THE DEAL

LEIGH GROSSMAN

NEW YORK

Copyright © 2001 LearningExpress, LLC.

All rights reserved under International and Pan-American Copyright Conventions. Published in the United States by LearningExpress, LLC, New York.

Library of Congress Cataloging-in-Publication Data:
Grossman, Leigh.
     Closing the deal/Leigh Ronald Grossman.
         p. cm.
     Includes index.
     ISBN 1-57685-360-8 (pbk.)
     1. Real estate listings—United States. 2. Real estate agents—United States. 3. Real estate business—United States. 4. Internet Marketing—United States. I. Title.

HD279 .G77 2001
333.33'068'8—dc21   00-051844

Printed in the United States of America
9 8 7 6 5 4
First Edition

For more information or to place an order, contact LearningExpress at:
900 Broadway
Suite 604
New York, NY 10003

Or visit us at:
www.learnatest.com

CONTENTS

THE EXPERT ADVISORS FOR THIS BOOK ARE:

RALPH TAMPER, DREI, CREI, GRI, CBR, Real Estate School, Houston, TX; president of the Real Estate Educators' Association

ED FARTHING, Broker Associate, Coldwell Banker George T. Decker, Binghamton, NY

PAT FARTHING, Broker Associate, Coldwell Banker George T. Decker, Binghamton, NY

RUSS HICKS, President, R. Sparrow-Hicks Real Estate, South Woodstock, CT

EXPERT ADVISORY PANEL

RALPH TAMPER

Ralph Tamper is President of the Real Estate Education Association. He is a nationally recognized authority in the real estate field as educator, trainer, and author. Additionally, he has written on subjects such as real estate mathematics and real estate contracts. His certifications include CBR (Certified Buyer Representative) and CREI (Certified Real Estate Instructor); he is also designated as DREI (Distinguished Real Estate Instructor) and GRI (Graduate REALTOR® Institute). Mr. Tamper is also Chairman of the Education and Member Profitability Task Force of the Houston Association of REALTORS® and a member of the National Association of REALTORS® Education Committee.

ED FARTHING

Ed Farthing, a licensed broker for 27 years and a licensed salesperson for 32 years, is an Associate Broker with Coldwell Banker George T. Decker Real Estate in Broome County, New York. He is licensed in both New York and Pennsylvania, and has sold, leased, built, renovated, appraised, and managed property throughout the region. Mr. Farthing is a member of The Broome County Board of REALTORS®, The New York State Association of REALTORS®, The National Association of REALTORS® and The New York State Commercial Association of REALTORS®.

PAT B. FARTHING

Pat Farthing is a licensed Real Estate Broker in Broome County, New York. She has been a broker for the past 15 years and a licensed salesperson for 23 years. She is presently an Associate Broker with Coldwell Banker George T. Decker Real Estate. She is a member of The Broome County Board of REALTORS®, The New York State Association of REALTORS® and The National Association of REALTORS®. She especially enjoys working with first time buyers and singles, giving them her utmost attention, patience, and guidance throughout the purchase process.

Pat and Ed Farthing are part of the Panel of Experts that produced *The Unofficial Guide to Buying a Home*, IDG, 1997. Together, they are consistently cited as Top Producers in their region.

RUSS HICKS

Russ Hicks is President of R. Sparrow Hicks Real Estate, located in South Woodstock, Connecticut and has been a licensed Connecticut broker for 27 years. He is also licensed in New York, Massachusetts, and Rhode Island and is a member of the Real Estate Educators Association. His certifications include ABR (Accredited Buyer Representative), CRB (Certified Residental Specialist), and GRI (Graduate REALTOR® Institute). Mr. Hicks' firm specializes in residential real estate in Northeastern Connecticut.

ACKNOWLEDGMENTS

Many REALTORS®, home buyers, sellers, and other people involved with real estate in one capacity or another were kind enough to speak with me and offer advice and useful information while I wrote this book. The following real estate agents and brokers were interviewed at length, and their advice for new agents forms the backbone of the book: Louise Barbee, Gayle Dinerstein, Roberta Dinerstein, Terry Kulka, and Pat Malek.

I would also like to thank Lesley McBain and Susan Sandberg-Diment from Swordsmith, Jason Schwartzberg and Margaret Piskitel at LearningExpress, and, most important, editor Jennifer Farthing.

REAL ESTATE SALES 101

◆ WHAT EXACTLY DOES A REAL ESTATE AGENT DO?

INTRODUCTION

As a residential real estate sales agent, your job is to negotiate an agreement between people who may not have much in common—home buyers and sellers. You are a sort of go-between, like a peace negotiator or a marriage broker. But unlike a peace negotiator, usually you are paid by only one side—the sellers, even if the sellers don't always understand what you're doing (and sometimes makes your job more difficult). Also unlike a negotiator, you don't get paid if you can't help the two sides reach an agreement.

Closing the Deal is a guide to the process of selling real estate. It's not just a book of sales tips (although there are plenty of sales tips here); it's a set of tools to help make your job—and your life—easier. *Closing the Deal* is designed to help you find buyers and sellers, to help you understand their needs (often better than your clients understand them), and to take you through the process of matching buyers and sellers with each other. The book is also designed to help you anticipate problems and handle them before they start—and to solve problems that can't be avoided without losing sales.

THE PROCESS OF SELLING A HOME

Selling real estate is a complicated process—so complicated that many new agents get confused or discouraged and never sell anything. It's a career that takes over the lives of many new agents completely. On the other hand, it also can be a lot of fun. You'll meet and get to know people you'd never encounter otherwise. And, there are a lot of people who are making a pretty good living at it and many who are making a *very good* living at it.

How do they do it?

Don't worry about them. This book's about you: how to put your skills to work, build a successful real estate career, and not sacrifice your sanity along the way.

You'll need to break the process of selling houses down into pieces. *Closing the Deal* walks you through each of those steps, drawing on the experiences of successful agents from around the country to help you avoid making the mistakes that make selling real estate so difficult for many new agents. There are sections dealing with getting listings, preparing sellers and their houses, finding and qualifying buyers, showing homes to different kinds of buyers, closing sales, and keeping sales from falling apart at the last minute. You'll also find troubleshooting material here—the answers to some of the unexpected problems and often sticky situations that crop up in real estate sales.

TYPES OF REPRESENTATION

As a real estate agent, you have an unusual relationship with your clients. The seller pays your bills, but satisfied buyers are one of the biggest sources of referrals—and are vital to your future income.

Until a few years ago, things were a lot clearer for real estate agents. The agent worked for the sellers. Period. The agent's job was to sell his or her client's house for the highest price possible. Buyers' agents were rare although not unheard of; most buyers had no one representing them in the real estate process.

The problem was that many buyers were only vaguely aware of this. While most states required buyers to read and sign real estate disclosure forms that explained the process in detail (although sometimes in confusing legalese), many buyers refused to believe that the friendly real estate agent driving them around, showing them houses, and helping them work things out with the bank wasn't working for them. They had an even harder time with the idea that their real estate agent—who was privy to all of their deepest financial secrets—actually represented sellers whom the agent might never have met.

Some of them sued.

As a result, a lot has changed in the way residential real estate is bought and sold over the last few years. While many agents still represent sellers exclusively, agents representing buyers and dual agents—who represent both buyers and sellers simultaneously—have become much more common. At different times you are likely to find yourself in all of these roles. And while your income (except in certain specified cases) still comes from the sellers, the potential for conflicts of interest and misunderstandings is much lower than it used to be.

Which doesn't mean that there aren't still a lot of unhappy buyers, sellers, and, for that matter, real estate agents. The key to avoiding all of those things is understanding the needs of your clients and your own abilities and strengths as an agent. This book is designed to help you in all of these areas— helping you to build on your strengths as an agent as well as providing some hard-and-fast tools to address areas in which you may not be as strong.

TRADITIONAL REPRESENTATION

Traditionally, real estate sales agents represent the sellers. People who want to sell houses agree to be listed by you—to have you as their exclusive selling agent for a period of time agreed to in a contract. When you sell the house, you get a portion of the profits (usually 5 or 6 percent), which will be split between you and the agency you work for if you're not an independent broker. (If you are particularly valuable to your agency, you will be able to negotiate a better percentage with it.) If another agent sells a house that you are listing, you split the commission with that agent (again giving part of your share to the agency).

If you work exclusively as a sellers' agent, any buyers you show houses to need to be made aware of that fact. While different states have different disclosure forms that are designed to make buyers aware of the nature of seller representation, you don't want to count on those forms to inform the buyers. If you're very clear up front with the buyers about what you can and can't do for them, they won't feel betrayed later.

Most agents mix traditional representation with buyer brokerage— where they are working exclusively for the buyers. However, if you're in an exceptionally fast-moving market—where a good listing sells within a week or two—you may choose to represent sellers only.

BUYER BROKERAGE

As a new agent, often it's easier to find potential buyers than sellers, so it's likely that you'll represent more buyers than sellers until you can build up listings of your own. As a buyer broker, you sign up potential buyers to the same sort of agreement that sellers sign—they agree that you will be their sole representative for a fixed period of time. (In some states this is done much more formally than in others; you may find yourself representing clients without a formal agreement in some areas.) After your clients decide on a house, you work with the sellers' agent to close the deal and split the selling agent's commission on the house.

Buyer brokerage allows buyers to feel that they have representation in buying a house—that there is someone on their side in what for most people is an enormous transaction. It also lowers the likelihood of conflicts of interest, since you aren't in the position of knowing confidential information from both sides in the transaction. For instance, if you feel a house is overpriced, you can say so and show the buyer why. On the other hand, because a second agent is involved, it cuts the size of your commission.

DUAL REPRESENTATION

It's not unusual for an agent to represent both the sellers and the buyers at the same time. One agent compares it to being a mother who has to balance the needs of two children. If one of your buyers is interested in a property for which you are the listing agent, you may legally represent both of them in most localities, but you will have to be very careful not to share confidential information from either side. You need not only to make the sale work but also to satisfy both parties that you have fulfilled their contracts with you. So even if you feel the sellers are asking too much for the house, you can't say so to the buyers. Likewise, even though you know how much the buyers are willing to spend for the property, you can't give that information to the sellers when you're presenting the buyers' offer.

As a dual agent, you represent the property honestly and fairly. The buyers decide what they want to pay, and the sellers decide what they want to sell it for. Your job is to negotiate anything in between.

SUMMING UP

To be successful as a residential real estate sales agent, you will need to develop techniques that work for you. This book is designed to help you build on your strengths as well as identify and address any shortcomings you may have as a new agent.

You may represent buyers, sellers, or both simultaneously. Most agents will combine all three types of representation.

LEARNING TO SELL YOURSELF

- As a new agent, how do you bring your own personal strengths to the job?

- How to assess your skills and bringing them to bear on the process of selling real estate

- The downside of starting out in a commission-based career

- The life of a real estate agent: working weekends and evenings

---

To be successful in real estate—especially as a new agent establishing yourself—you need to make a total commitment to the job. In many ways, you're just like the owner of any other start-up business who has to work long hours to establish your business—except the product you're selling is not just houses but your own skills, expertise, and personality.

Many new real estate agents don't realize the level of commitment involved. Whenever the real estate market is booming, there's a flood of new agents who think they can make very large incomes without the hard work that comes with those incomes. Many of those new agents last only a year or so before dropping out of the field, bewildered at their failure to sell properties.

Houses don't sell themselves. You need to put as much work into your real estate career as you would into any start-up business. If you're not prepared to work nights and weekends, in all kinds of weather, you won't be successful. If you don't take the time to do your homework—to understand the neighborhoods where you're selling and what's special about them, the procedures you need to follow in your area, and to research the houses you're showing—you won't be successful. If you're not familiar with your own strengths and abilities as an agent—what you bring to the job and how to turn those abilities into sales—you won't be successful.

On the other hand, if you are prepared—if you come to the field with a willingness to do what it takes to satisfy your clients and a desire to be successful—you're likely to do very well. It may take a while, but you will succeed.

MARKETING YOURSELF

The key to selling real estate is to jump in head first. You can't wait until you're perfect at it or until the perfect listing opportunity comes along. You just have to jump in and start working. Will you make mistakes? Will you embarrass yourself? Absolutely, but you'll learn from those experiences, learn to fix the mistakes—and some of those embarrassing opening moments will turn into sales down the road.

How do you go about selling yourself? It's not enough just to print out some cards and hand them out. You won't succeed just by memorizing some sales techniques or a phone script. You have to get in touch with what's important about the job to you. To be effective, you have to be passionate about selling real estate, just as a teacher or a lawyer needs to be passionate to be effective. It's not enough to know your material; you have to show clients that you care about your job—and about *them*.

This book contains many different ideas about how to connect with people and build clientele. But here are some places to get started on marketing yourself. Ask yourself the following questions:

✓   Have you talked to your family about what you're doing? Do *all* your family members know that you're a real estate sales agent looking for clients now? Have you asked family members if they know anyone looking to buy or sell a house in your area? Do their friends? Don't assume you already know the answers just because they're your family. Don't be afraid to ask your family members to ask *their* friends. Chances are pretty good that one of your aunt's friends has a sister who's planning on moving out of state and needs to sell her house.

✓ Do your friends know that you want them to keep an eye out for potential clients and actively refer them to you? A lot of people only have a hazy idea of how real estate sales work, especially if they've never bought or sold houses. You need to enlighten them and get your friends to ask *their* friends and family if they know of anyone planning on buying or selling a house in your area.

✓ Do you keep in touch with other friendly acquaintances who would be happy to help? What about old high school teachers or former employers who you're still on good terms with?

✓ Are there people you do business with regularly who come into contact with a lot of other people? Who fixes your car? Who mows your lawn? How well do you know your mail carrier and newspaper carrier? All of these people are potential sources of clients—and some of them may be potential clients as well.

WHY AGENTS FAIL

I remember one person who took her training with me. She appeared to have a lot of potential: She looked professional, she was intelligent, she was poised, she had a command of the language, she had a pleasant, easy-to-listen-to speaking voice, and she had an effervescence about her, a bubbliness. But about six or seven months later the broker who had hired her told me that this woman had asked her to send her license back to the state. The broker said, "Where are you going to work?" She said, "Well, I've got a job at the department store." The broker said, "Well, surely they don't pay as much as real estate." "Yeah, but I need a regular job with a steady income. I need a real job." The broker looked her square in the eye and said, "If you'd worked this like a real job, you'd have more money than you'd know what to do with."

It's not enough to obtain your license and have the outward appearance of a professional—you have to be proactive to find listings, and you must approach this career as carefully and conscientiously as any other, perhaps even more so. You work hard, you follow through, and you make your own success. It's not likely to happen overnight, but if you remain dedicated, it will happen.

—RALPH TAMPER, The Real Estate School, Houston, Texas

THE DOWNSIDE FOR NEW AGENTS

Just because the real estate market is hot now doesn't mean it will stay that way. A good real estate agent will be able to succeed in a slow market—but to ensure that success, you need to lay the groundwork now. Don't be surprised if it takes a while to get going. Becoming successful takes time—and if you're banking on a huge amount of income right at the start, you're probably in for an unpleasant surprise.

As Pat Malek, a broker with First Choice Realty in Connecticut, remembers, "Being a REALTOR® is very expensive. And I didn't realize it would be as challenging as it is. It's important to be prepared." Before you start your real estate career, you should have enough income saved to cover your basic living expenses for six months. Even if you are able to sell properties right away, it could take a couple of months from the time you put a buyer and seller together until you receive your first commission check. Here are some basic expenses to factor in:

✓ **New clothes**—You will need to dress professionally all the time, not just occasionally. Even your casual clothes need to be presentable, because everyone you meet is a potential new client. Don't forget good shoes—ones that stay comfortable after a full day of walking around with clients.

✓ **Car expenses**—You will be putting a lot of mileage on your car, and it must be in perfect running order at all times. In many ways, your car is an extension of your office, since you will be using it to ferry buyers to see properties. Check your insurance policy to ensure that you have proper coverage. Expect your maintenance costs to go up substantially. Don't assume that gas prices won't go up, either, since you'll be refilling your tank a lot more often. You'll also want a roadside service, such as AAA; you don't want to lose clients because you couldn't get a minor breakdown fixed while you were showing them houses—costing them hours of their time unnecessarily and making them question your competence.

✓ **Flyers and handouts**—You will be printing flyers and other handouts to give people as you seed neighborhoods or use other techniques to build your client base. This will probably cost at least $1,000; most likely, more. For more information on flyers and other promotions, see Chapter 3.

✓ **Fees and memberships**—You will be actively socializing with other people as part of your work. Don't forget to budget for dues and memberships fees.

✓ **Childcare**—If you have children, you can't take them with you when you show houses, even if you work from home. You need to have reliable childcare that's available on a moment's notice.

✓ **Office supplies**—Even if you're with an agency that handles routine office supplies, you will need to make sure you have what you need to keep track of your clients at all times. That may mean a personal computer, a Palm™ handheld, or Day-Timer®, or some other combination of organizing systems—but all of them cost money.

✓ **Eating out**—You will need to entertain clients at times, and you'll be eating a lot of lunches from the road. If you're eating out with a client, you don't want to appear impoverished (or just cheap) or you're going to have a hard time achieving success.

✓ **Cell phone and/or pager**—Your clients need to be able to reach you at all times, and you need to be able to call people back from wherever you happen to be. Even with a good calling plan, cell phones can be expensive. Make certain you budget for a high volume of calls.

✓ **Food and basic necessities**—You need to be realistic in budgeting for household expenses, especially if you have a family. If your plan for succeeding in real estate requires you to live austerely for six months, you're not going to enjoy the job much—and you need to enjoy your work to be successful at selling real estate.

✓ **Things you no longer have time to do**—With your time tied up in your career, you may find yourself having to pay for things you would have done yourself in the past. You may not have time to mow the lawn or clean out the gutters anymore. You may not have time to do that oil change on the car yourself. You may find yourself sending out the laundry with the dry cleaning.

SUPPORT STRUCTURES

It's important to have a support structure in place when you begin selling real estate. You will need to have people to turn to in the months ahead, and you'll need to prepare them for what you will be going through—and what you'll be putting them through. You don't want to alienate your family and friends when you'll need them the most. To succeed, you're going to make a big commitment of both time and energy—including some of the energy that you may have used for your family, friends, or significant other. If the people who are important in your life aren't prepared for what the first months of your real estate career will bring, it can lead to problems. It's important that you have their help, support, and understanding—especially in the initial stages of your career where you're hearing a lot of no's for every yes.

One veteran broker cautions, "Real estate can take its toll on new agents' families and significant others. When agents start out in real estate, they aren't home for dinner and they are often away on weekends. They aren't making any money, and they start to wonder after a while whether this was a great decision and whether all the expenses for the car and eating those frozen dinners was worth it. They need a lot of support." Some things to keep in mind:

✓ Do everything you can to enlist the support of your friends and family in advance. Let them know what to expect. Ask for their help and support. If there's anything specific you want help with, ask for it ahead of time. The more your friends and family feel like they're part of a team helping you to succeed, the more they'll be willing to do. Don't be afraid to ask your friends for help, for contacts, and for information. People who care about you will be happy to help as long as they don't feel taken advantage of; what they don't want is to be ignored or feel you no longer care about them.

✓ Give people a time line. People who care about you will be willing to make accommodations for you if they know it's not permanent. If you're going to be inconsistent about making it to traditional family events for the next year, let people know in advance. People will be hurt when you fail to do the things that you've always done; however, if you let them know what to expect, it will be a pleasant surprise when you *can* make it.

✓ When planning your time, don't forget that your commitments go beyond the hours spent at the office or showing properties. You need to spend time reading and researching, traveling around neighborhoods, taking courses, and participating in other activities.

✓ Make time just for your family and friends. No matter how busy you are—and you will be very busy—you can always put aside a little time to spend with the people who care about you. It may be just a brief get-together with a friend for coffee between appointments, but it will remind people that you still care enough to make an effort to see them—and it will help you stay connected with the rest of your life and the people who care about you at a time when you have to be obsessive about your career.

✓ Make time to exercise. You'll be running around all the time; you need to be energetic and in shape. This can be especially important because you're going to have trouble keeping to a good diet while you're showing houses and shuttling people around town. You may end up eating at a lot of drive-through and fast food meals.

✓ Make a little time for yourself, too. You can't work all the time. Every once in a while you need to give yourself a few hours when it's okay not to worry about anything or put too much pressure on yourself.

THE BIG PICTURE

Don't lose sight of why you went into the field, or what real estate has to offer—money, excitement, constant new challenges, and a fast-paced environment. As much of a cliché as it may be, you need to keep a positive attitude. There will be times when you're lucky or unlucky, but more than almost any other field, your success in real estate is based on how much you put into it.

Remember the following points in the first few months while you're struggling to balance your time and stretch your energy to the limits.

✓ Real estate may take you away from family and friends more than you like during the first few months, but it brings you in touch with many other people. You will meet interesting and stimulating people with whom you never otherwise would have come into contact, and will make friendships that will last for the rest of your life.

✓ Unlike most other careers, in real estate your success is largely dependent on your efforts. While you may have years when you're especially lucky or unlucky, by and large your income and success are directly related to your own motivation and drive. You'll never have to feel that an incompetent boss is underutilizing you or that you'll never get ahead in your salaried job, no matter how hard you work or how many long hours you invest.

Real estate is a career, but remember to keep sight of your goals as you enter the field. Do you have specific money goals? Do you want to be comfortable and have time for your family and friends, or is it more important to you to be wealthy enough to retire early? You probably entered the field with specific long-term goals; you don't want to lose sight of those goals because of the intensity of your first year as a real estate sales agent.

In addition to your ultimate goals, you want to have a good idea of what strengths and personality traits you bring to the field and how you can use them to help make your first months as an agent more successful and less stressful.

Your Strengths

What are some of the strengths you bring to the field? Now is the time for an honest assessment of your strengths and weaknesses as a salesperson. We'd all like to think that first impressions don't count, but in real estate if you can't make a passable first impression, you may never have a chance to let people see your real skills.

There are a few key strengths that help a real estate agent land clients. Nobody has all of them; what you want to do is make use of the ones you're best at while developing the others.

✓ **Phone manner**—How do you sound on the phone? Do people open up to you easily? Are you comfortable talking with near strangers? Do you squeak when you get nervous? If you're very comfortable and/or come off well on the phone, you may have an easier time making cold calls and may be able to make many initial arrangements by phone. If you're not, arrange to meet with people in person initially. You will get more comfortable as you make more calls, no matter how nervous you are now. You may never want to make cold calls, but with experience even the most phone-shy agent can become smoother on the phone.

✓ **Appearance**—What sort of first impression do you make when people see you? This isn't about looks; it's about grooming, appropriate dress, and body language. It's important to look successful and dress in a way that shows respect for your clients (as well as common sense—dress nicely, but don't wear high heels if you're walking buyers through eighteenth-century attics). Try not to look or act nervous, but don't make a big deal out of a slight case of nerves; people won't hold it against you. Wear clothes that make you feel both confident and comfortable.

That said, if you're not sure what sort of first impression you make, find one or two people whose opinions you respect (and who fit the demographics of home buyers in your area) and ask them what they think. And listen to them, even if it's not what you want to hear.

✓ **Self-confidence**—Confidence sells. If you sound as if you know what you're talking about, people will believe you, while if you sound uncertain, they'll question your every word. If you come off as nervous or uncertain, you really have to do your homework before you meet with a client, so you have the answers at your fingertips.

Most of all, your clients care about your ability to close a real estate deal successfully. Everything else is secondary to them. Does that mean no one will ever have a problem with you for reasons beyond your control? Of course not, but that person's not going to be a successful sale anyway; worrying about it will only negatively affect your potentially successful sales.

✓ **Tact**—Do you come off as pleasant and polite, or are you always saying the wrong thing? Do you always mediate your friends' fights, or do you accidentally start them? If you're not the most tactful person in the world, get used to watching people's body language for cues. If you say something wrong, you need to be able to fix it quickly; if you don't, it can cost you thousands of dollars in a single lost commission. Also, watch out for words or phrases that seem innocuous but can be offensive; when in doubt, hold your tongue.

✓ **Attention to detail**—How good are you at keeping track of details and loose ends? There are a lot of loose ends in real estate, and home buyers and sellers, who are going through a nerve-wracking process, can be disorganized. Being organized by nature is a real asset; you'll be able to keep everything on schedule and help keep frantic buyers and sellers on schedule, as well. Being organized will make you feel more confident, too.

If you're not naturally organized, now is the time to come up with a system. Get in the habit of *writing everything down*, even if it doesn't seem important. Start keeping notes on all phone calls and conversations with clients and potential clients. Keep this information sorted out so you can easily find what you need; it doesn't have to be a database, as long as the system works for you.

It may seem like a lot of work, but the first time you misplace a note and it costs you a $9,000 commission, you'll feel differently.

✓ **Energy level**—Are you a morning person? Are you always tired at 3:00 P.M.? Do you come across as peppy, or are you naturally languid? As a real estate agent, you want to be aware of your energy levels—and your clients'. If you're always tired at a certain time of day, either avoid scheduling appointments for that time, or do something to bring up your energy level right before the meeting. (Nutritionists would recommend a brisk walk instead of a Snickers bar, but do whatever works for you.) If you start to snap at people whenever your blood sugar gets low, drink some juice before you sit down with your clients.

By the same token, if your clients seem like they're about to fall over or aren't hearing a word you're saying, it's probably a good time to suggest stopping for coffee, instead of plunging into the details of the next house you're planning to show them.

Another piece of advice. If you're naturally low key, it's okay; don't try to pretend you have a different personality. Clients will buy and sell houses through a real estate agent who is low key yet genuine. However, they rarely buy from an agent who comes off as fake or insincere. Remember, this is a major purchase for the customer, not a day's work. They expect honesty—not someone who simply tells them what they want to hear.

✓ **Language**—In addition to your speaking voice, pay attention to the *way* you speak. Tape record yourself talking for a few minutes and play the tape back: How many *umm*s and *er*s and *like*s do you hear? Get out of the habit of using filler words when you speak. If you have a strong regional or foreign accent, make certain you'll be understandable to your clients; you must be sure your clients are paying attention to what you're saying rather than just the sound of your voice.

✓ **Vehicle**—You're going to have a lot of people riding in your car. It doesn't have to be the most expensive car in the world, but it does need to be clean and reliable. If your car doesn't feel safe and comfortable in the weather conditions in which you're selling houses, you're not going to be able to convince clients to buy in, say, a New England winter.

Take a good look at your car as a stranger (or new client) would see it. Are there conspicuous dents that give the impression that you're not a safe driver? Are there bumper stickers espousing political causes that might make a client uncomfortable? From a client's point of view, a real estate agent's car is an extension of that agent.

Just as important, don't let your excitement about the property you're showing cause you to take your eyes off the road. Focus not just on driving well, but on driving in a way that makes your passengers comfortable in the car with you. Be aware of your driving style and tone it down if necessary when you have clients in the car. If they think you're a reckless driver, they're likely to think you're a reckless real estate agent as well.

✓ **Accessibility**—Being accessible, easily available, and convenient to reach goes a long way with potential customers. Get a reliable cell phone or pager. Check your messages frequently and return calls right away—even if it's just to set up a time to talk later. Remember that buying or selling a home is a huge emotional and financial investment for your clients, and many of them will call frequently with not-very-important questions, sometimes just for reassurance that they're doing the right thing. If you can stay patient, helpful, sympathetic, and at least somewhat cheerful with clients when they call at all hours, you're likely to be successful.

✓ **Sensitivity to scents**—Do you use heavy fragrances or aftershave? Are you a smoker? A lot of people are very sensitive—or even allergic—to fragrances or cigarette smoke. If you choose to wear a fragrance or aftershave, go easy—a little goes a long way. Likewise, keep breath mints handy for those times when you don't have the opportunity to brush your teeth. Never chew gum.

If you smoke, don't ever do it in the room where you meet with clients, in your car (where you will be traveling with clients), or around paperwork that you will be giving to clients. (Paper absorbs and retains smoke.) And avoid smoking immediately before meeting with clients. It's tough to make a sale when your client is sensitive to smoke.

THINGS TO KEEP IN YOUR CAR

• First aid kit with bandages, pain relievers, and other essentials to keep a minor cut or blister from ruining your day (or your client's)

+ A few toys, books, and drawing paper and crayons. Some clients will bring children with them, and you'll want the kids to be entertained and not cranky. Keep the supplies in a small box for neatness.
+ Several umbrellas—enough for you and your clients if it begins raining unexpectedly.
+ Spare shoes or boots and socks in case yours get wet. If you're female, keep spare panty hose in the car.
+ Maps—keep a road atlas and street maps of the area handy. You never know when you're going to have to make an unexpected detour because of road construction, or when you'll find yourself on an unfamiliar and poorly marked road.
+ Recent real estate listing books or brochures, to give clients something to look through while you're driving. Get in the habit of putting the previous week's listings in your car whenever the new listings come in.
+ Pad and pens for clients to take notes on if they forget writing materials

---

TIME MANAGEMENT

Being a real estate agent is extremely demanding of your time. Essentially, you are at work around the clock. Every client is going to think he or she is your main priority—and to be effective, you want each of your clients to feel like that he or she has your full attention, even though you may have many clients at a time. Clients probably won't realize if you're tired or overworked, and if they think you're taking on too much, they'll go elsewhere. You need to be able to juggle multiple clients at once and to keep the rest of your life—and your sanity—intact while doing it.

Some ways to make the most of your time:

✓ Be realistic in your scheduling. Don't design a jam-packed schedule, or you'll find yourself running late all day.

✓ Make sure the easy stuff is taken care of. You're always going to have a couple of unexpected crises every week. The key to keeping things running is to make sure all the easy, routine things are handled and running on time. If the easy stuff is taken care of, you'll have time to deal with the crises. If it isn't, then the routine things will turn into problems while you're handling the emergencies.

✓ Make calls when you're fresh. Try to make calls when your energy level is high. It's easier to be energetic when there are people in front of you than it is over the phone.

✓ Don't waste time on the phone. Keep chitchat to a minimum; be friendly, but don't fall into the trap of spending fifteen minutes on a three-minute call. Those fifteen-minute calls add up in a hurry.

✓ Keep things organized so you can find them. You may never have the neatest desk in the world, but make sure you know where to find everything—and that means *everything*. You don't want to waste time or be late for appointments because you can't find a crucial piece of paper.

✓ Ask for help when you need it. If you don't have time to mow the lawn or make an elaborate dinner, or do any of the other household tasks you're used to completing, get someone else to do them (hire someone if you need to) instead of promising yourself that you'll make time to do them somehow.

✓ Occasionally reward yourself for getting things accomplished. Remember that real estate may be stressful, but it's fun, too. You're no good to your clients or yourself if you never have any time for yourself. Don't be afraid to reward yourself if you've had a particularly productive stretch of time.

✓ Know your limits. Be aware when you're getting in over your head and need to step back. You need to drive yourself hard, but not into a nervous breakdown. Push yourself as hard as you can, but if you're feeling stressed out and irritable, get some rest. You can always take a short nap and then get back to work.

EXPECTATIONS

What should you expect to get out of real estate, in return for all the time and effort and emotion you're putting into it?

✓ **Excitement**—You may be stressed, but you'll never be bored. The job changes from day to day and moment to moment. Real estate is challenging and fast-paced. You'll switch gears frequently, instead of doing the same thing for long enough for it to get boring or routine.

✓ **People**—You'll work with many different kinds of people, and you'll be meeting new faces constantly. If you like to interact with people, real estate is a terrific field.

✓ **Satisfaction**—Unlike most sales jobs, you're helping people purchase something they want and, in many cases, you're helping people to improve their lives dramatically. There's a real satisfaction in helping buyers to find and purchase their dream house or helping sellers to better themselves financially.

✓ **Money**—Once you're established, real estate can be a lucrative field. Even a hardworking newcomer can make reasonably good money. According to Ralph Tamper, "The first year if you really work hard, you might earn $35,000 or $36,000. I've seen people earn a great deal more, but I've seen people not even approach that. An income of $35,000 to $40,000 is a realistic expectation. If you accomplish that the first year, then I think it's realistic to think that you might be able to double that in the second year, because then you've got approaches and techniques and you're beginning to do the job well. A lot of people think they're going to earn $100,000 the first year. In most markets, It's probably not going to happen."

But a lot of other things *will* happen as you begin the process of finding sellers and buyers, showing homes, and closing real estate deals.

SUMMING UP

There's plenty of money in real estate, but you'll have to work hard to get it, and you should expect to put in many, many hours until you get established. Many real estate agents fail because they don't realize how much work is involved or because they have unrealistic expectations about their first-year income.

Be aware of how you present yourself and of your strengths and weaknesses as a communicator. A lot of your initial success depends on your ability to play up your strengths while you gain enough experience to overcome any weaknesses you might have.

The biggest key to success is just to jump in and do it. If you worry too much about potential pitfalls and mistakes, you'll never get started.

UNDERSTANDING THE SELLERS

+ How does a new agent find sellers and convert them to listings?

+ How do you turn customers' unrealistic expectations into a successful real estate partnership?

+ What are the best ways to prepare homes for sale?

You might think of selling a house as just a business transaction between two parties that you are brokering, but that's not what the seller thinks. Even the most businesslike sellers are emotionally attached to the house they are selling—no matter what they say. Sellers are selling a part of their lives.

Part of your job is to help sellers through that process. The more comfortable you make sellers, the more helpful they will be. Uncomfortable sellers may actually obstruct a sale, consciously or unconsciously. But no matter how difficult some sellers may be to work with—many sellers are a pleasure to work with—always remember that *sellers control your income*. (Even agents who work only as buyer brokers earn their commissions from sellers, just less directly.) You don't get paid if you don't sell the sellers' house. Actually, you lose on an unsold house: You lose all the money you spent advertising, all the time you spent showing the house, and the goodwill of the unsatisfied sellers—which might have gone into referrals and new clients.

You'll also want to keep in mind that most people who are selling their houses are also *buying* another house. Therefore, most sellers are buyers, as well. If sellers are not leaving the area, you may be able to handle both sales.

SOME TECHNIQUES FOR FINDING SELLERS

- **Cold calls**—Call people in a neighborhood to find out if they're interested in selling or know someone who might be interested
- **Farming a neighborhood**—Blanket a neighborhood with information about yourself so that people interested in selling houses remember your name and have a positive image of you
- **Open houses**—People who are selling houses often visit open houses to see how other houses in their area are being marketed
- **Organizations**—If you're involved in activities and community organizations, you'll be in contact with many people who share interests with you—some of whom will be selling houses or will know people who are
- **Expired listings**—Sometimes it's worth taking a shot at a property that another real estate agent has failed to sell
- **Referrals**—People you know might have a house to sell, or they might know someone else who does

---

FINDING SELLERS

Conventional wisdom dictates that an established agent relies on referrals from past customers to get new customers. Therefore, a new agent would have to make cold calls in order to find new customers—*lots* of cold calls. However, in many areas of the United States, cold calls just aren't very effective anymore. In fact, many agencies discourage new agents from making cold calls. And unless you're really good at calling people (or you're in an area where cold calls are likely to be successful), you may want to use your time and energy on more effective techniques for finding sellers, such as mining your friends and relatives and building a broad network of contacts in the neighborhoods where you work.

One of the biggest mistakes new agents make is to neglect the people they already know. You've probably already thought of your friends and relatives, but you need to make certain that your friends talk to *their* friends, too. Don't just take it for granted that everyone you know remembers that you have a real estate license and are looking for clients. And people with whom you have a personal connection—whether they're friends of friends, people you do business with, your neighbors, or people you've met while waiting in line or sitting on a bus—are better clients than people you've met through cold calling or spreading flyers through a neighborhood. They're likely to be more trusting and less suspicious; you can spend more time selling their house and less time allaying their fears.

A few things to remember:

✓ You're a real estate agent 24 hours a day. Never stop looking for leads. Even when you're shopping for groceries or doing your laundry, be on the lookout for potential clients or for places to advertise.

✓ Every person you do business with is a potential supplier of leads to you. Your child's teacher, your banker, your insurance agent, your accountant, your veterinarian, your dry cleaner, your printer—all of them may know someone who is selling or buying a house.

✓ Don't let potential clients slip away without asking them if they know someone who's planning on selling or buying a house. You have to ask everyone you talk with if they're considering buying or selling a home, or if they know someone else who is.

✓ Learn to ask people about real estate without sounding intrusive. People who are interested in buying or selling houses *want* to talk about it. Other people won't be offended by what amounts to work chitchat or by your expression of interest in them. Nobody's going to be upset when you ask "Do you know anybody who's looking?" as long as you do it in a friendly, appropriate way. And it shouldn't be the *only* thing you say to someone, or they will be put off.

Even as a brand-new agent, chances are most of your listings will come through referrals. You just have to work a little harder to get referrals than an established agent, who has years of practice at talking with people about real estate. Here are some techniques to generate sellers that work for other agents.

COLD-CALL TECHNIQUES

Some agents like to make cold calls, and they can be effective in some areas. For one reason or another, you may have no other way of getting clients. You may work in an area where people are less put off by phone solicitations. Or you may be really good on the phone and eager to put your skills to good use.

Real estate buyers and sellers are increasingly savvy. You need to do your homework and know the potential clients' neighborhood before you start calling if you want to have any chance of success. Some suggestions to get started:

✓ Drive around the neighborhood first to familiarize yourself with it. Even if it's an area you know well, drive around it again and think about the neighborhood from the viewpoint of someone who might be buying or selling a home.

✓ Use a street directory to get numbers in a particular neighborhood. If you don't have easy access to a street directory or reverse phone directory, there are free directories available over the Internet, such as the one at www.anywho.com/telq.html.

✓ Don't call people too early in the morning (before 9:00 or 10:00 A.M.) or in the evening when people are just getting home or are eating dinner (between 7:00 and 9:00 is okay, but don't call any later than 9:00).

✓ Don't call on religious holidays or during special events coverage (check the calendar to make sure it's not a major religious holiday you're not familiar with) or during major sporting events like the World Series or Super Bowl. Likewise, don't schedule your calls during presidential debates or major state of the union broadcasts.

✓ Be prepared to make a lot of calls at once. Don't take breaks between every call or give up after a few calls. Make at least ten calls before taking a break.

✓ Plan what you're going to say. You'll want to be comfortable on the phone and not sound stilted. You should have two scripts in front of you when you start calling: one for answering machines and one to get you started if someone answers the phone. Tailor the scripts to the neighborhood you're calling. Practice reading the script a few times until you're comfortable with it.

✓ Expect the first few calls to be a little awkward until you get a rhythm going. Don't be embarrassed if the first few calls aren't as smooth as you like; keep going until you're comfortable.

✓ Keep some hard candies or lozenges handy so you don't get hoarse. You may want to have a cup of tea or something soothing when you take your break. Avoid coffee, chocolate, and other harsh-on-the-throat items while making calls.

✓ Sit up straight in your chair while you're calling. Your voice will sound better and your back won't be sore after hours of calling. If you don't have a chair that will be comfortable for hours of calls, get one. You may want to invest in a phone headset as well if you make a lot of cold calls.

✓ Always thank people for their time, and give them your name and phone number before you get off the phone. You want to be polite and leave a good impression. Many people who aren't interested in selling a home when you call will need a real estate agent six months later, or will have a friend or relative who needs one. You want to leave them with the impression that you're friendly, competent, and easy to work with.

✓   Don't take rejection personally. People are geared to say no to telemarketers, and many people will say no before they've heard what you have to say. Some of them will be rude. It may take a while before you find any callers who are interested, even if you're doing everything right.

COLD CALL SCRIPT STARTERS

BASIC SCRIPT

"Hi, I'm _____ from _____ Realty. Is this _____? I was driving through your neighborhood and I think it's really beautiful. I was wondering if you might know of anyone who's thinking of selling their house, or if you've given any thought to selling your house. . . ."

> *Add or change material to highlight features of the neighborhood and emphasize what a special place it is.*

"You know, the lake is so beautiful, and I think that . . ."
"I love the view from the hills, and the way the land rolls . . ."
"The light through the leaves is so pretty this time of year . . ."

> *If the houses are what's significant about the neighborhood, mention them; if you know the particular house you're calling, say something positive about it.*

"I love all the big old Victorians . . ."

"I think your house is really beautiful, and I know that there are people who are looking for unusual homes."

"There are always people who are looking for important homes, especially now that people are trading up. . . ."

> *Express other people's interest in the neighborhood, but avoid stretching the truth.*

"I have a customer who's interested in buying a house in your neighborhood, and I was wondering if you know anyone who might be interested in selling their home."

SAMPLE COLD-CALL RESPONSES

IF THE CALLER SAYS . . .	*RESPOND WITH . . .*
"Oh, no, I love my house, I'm never leaving!"	"It's such a beautiful neighborhood, I wouldn't want to leave either if I lived there. But I was wondering if you know anyone else who might be thinking of selling their house . . . maybe someone who's planning on moving to a bigger house?" *If the person suggests someone, move on to the next item. If not, politely thank him or her. Be sure to give out your name and phone number in case the person thinks of someone who might be interested.*
"I think the guy down the block might be thinking of selling."	"Do you know his name?" *If not, get the address. Ask why the person you're talking to thinks the neighbor might be selling. (This is*

all information you can use when you call the neighbor.) Be certain to thank the person you're talking to for the information and give your name and phone number again in case they think of anybody else.

"We've been thinking about it. I wonder what my house is worth...."

"I'd be happy to talk with you more about it. It doesn't cost you anything to find out what your house is worth and what some other houses in your neighborhood have sold for recently. When would be a good time to meet?" *Make certain to get complete contact information before you get off the line and to give the prospective client your name and phone number. Continue to be upbeat and encouraging for the rest of the call.*

"This is a bad time."

"I'm sorry to disturb you. Is there a better time to call?—I'll only need a minute or two of your time." *If the caller stays hostile, politely thank him or her and get off the phone. Don't leave your name and number.*

"How did you get this number?"

"I've been calling everyone on your block, to see if anyone in your area is interested in selling. Can you think of anyone who's planning on selling their house?" *If the caller stays hostile, politely thank him or her and get off the phone. Don't leave your name and number.*

FARMING A NEIGHBORHOOD

Another traditional technique, farming a neighborhood, can still be successful—with modern updates, of course. Direct mail, flyers, and even door-to-door contact all can work, if they're tailored carefully to a particular neighborhood, and to your strengths as a communicator. According to Ralph Tamper, "I think city cold calls are pretty useless. A personal sphere of influence, personal contacts, and asking friends, colleagues, relatives, former work associates, anybody you know, for business and referrals is by far the best way to find clients today. If you geographically work a neighborhood, the farming concept still works. A sphere of influence is a form of farming, too. It's not a geographic farm, but farming is planting seeds and nurturing and keeping in contact. Some people you're going to have to communicate with by mail, and creating an e-mail newsletter is a great thing to do now."

Leaving flyers or cards at local businesses, on supermarket bulletin boards, or even in mailboxes or doorways in a selected neighborhood can build your name recognition and help you find both buyers and sellers. (See pages 56–58 for how to put together a flyer.) Many local businesses offer a communication networking area, such as a bulletin board. Places you might leave flyers or cards include the following (remember always to ask permission):

antique shops	insurance agencies
assisted living facilities	Kiwanis Club
banks	Library
bars/pubs	Lions Club
car dealers	military base
car washes	movers
chambers of commerce	nail salons
church	nursing homes
coffeeshops	Rotary Club
country clubs	school
day care centers	shopping mall

delicatessens	specialty stores
dry cleaners	supermarket
flea markets	synagogue
florists	tourism offices
gyms/exercise clubs	town halls
hairdressers/barbershops	university housing offices
human resources departments	veterinarians
at large corporations	

FINDING A NEIGHBORHOOD TO CALL

I did a lot of cold calling when I started out. My sister-in-law was also a real estate agent, and we knew a lot of the same people, and she had already contacted them. So I was forced to find other ways, and cold calling worked for me. I think that if you make calls in a specific area with really interesting homes, it can be effective.

I used to drive around and houses used to almost speak to me. Sometimes people have a lot of stuff, like furniture, out on garbage day, and sometimes it means they're thinking about selling. At other times I would just think, "I would love to be the listing agent on that property because it's an interesting house." Or I just thought an area was really nice. I used to just drive around until I found an area that I wanted to call.

—GAYLE DINERSTEIN, real estate agent,
Prudential Wykagyl-Rittenberg,
New Rochelle, New York

PIGGYBACK ON SOMEONE ELSE'S OPEN HOUSE

You'd be surprised at how many potential sellers come to open houses, to see how other homes in their area are being marketed. This is one of the first things many sellers do in researching the sales process. People often stop by an open house while they're still thinking about whether to sell—and before they've decided on a real estate agent. Open houses are also a way for potential sellers to audition real estate agents. They will talk to the agent and see if they can build a rapport, and then see how effectively the agent is marketing the open house.

As a new agent, you may want to see if an established agent in your office wants help covering an open house for one of his or her listings. Basically, you're trading your time (which the established agent won't have to spend at the open house) for any potential referrals that turn up. Of course, open houses are a rich source for potential buyers, too. If a buyer comes in and doesn't like the house she sees, ask some questions about what kind of home she does have in mind. Think about some listings in the area, give her your card, and encourage her to call you to go around looking at houses the following Saturday. Always take her name, too, so that you can follow up with a phone call and suggest a time to schedule a meeting.

Ed Farthing, broker associate at Coldwell Banker George T. Decker in Binghamton, New York, points out, "About 70 percent of the buyers who attend an open house have a house to sell. Find out if they've listed with an agency. If they haven't, encourage them to take your business card and call you for a free market analysis on their property. You stand a pretty good chance at becoming their listing agent. And, assuming they're not interested in the open house, you can always offer to show them some other properties in the region that might interest them."

At every open house, keep a sign-in book. The listing agent will be interested in this information, and you can use it to follow up with potential customers, too.

BELONG TO ORGANIZATIONS

Your hobbies, outside interests, and political affiliation are all fertile sources for new clients. Make certain that people with whom you socialize know that you're looking for clients. And as a new agent who may not be comfortable dealing with total strangers yet, it gives you a source of contacts you have something in common with—and something to talk about with, if the conversation turns awkward or you find yourself unsure of what to say next.

For instance, if you play a lot of tennis, you'll make contacts at your tennis club. If you're active in social or civic organizations, such as volunteer firefighters, the Audubon Society, the Red Cross, or the Lions Club, you can get some very good, qualified leads. The same is true of political organizations such as the League of Women Voters, Greenpeace, or local affiliates of the major political parties.

If you get a referral through a group you belong to that leads to a sale, you may want to make a donation to that group in honor of the person who listed with you. For example, if a fellow PTA member sells her house through you, you would make a donation to the elementary school in that person's name. You get good publicity when you're listed in the newsletter, you help a good cause, and other members will remember your generosity and be quick to recommend you to their friends and relatives.

Don't join organizations just for the contacts, though—it's a waste of your time and people will see through your intentions. Participate in groups that organize activities you enjoy or that foster philosophies you agree with, or become more active in organizations you already belong to. Just be careful not to spread yourself so thin with organizational activities that you don't have enough time left to go out and sell real estate.

EXPIRED LISTINGS

One easy way to get listings—not the best listings perhaps, but listings nonetheless—is to take on listings that have expired without selling. There's a fair chance that there's some sort of problem with these listings (or they would have sold already), but it may be a problem you can solve that the previous agent couldn't. Sellers who insisted on overpricing the house may be willing to lower the price now, for instance. Sometimes the problem is a personality conflict with the former agent, and you may find sellers with a reputation for unreasonableness to be pleasant and easy to deal with.

But be sure to do a little homework before saddling yourself with a possibly unsalable listing. Were the owners actively obstructing the sale? Is the house in poor condition, or located across the street from a newly constructed waste disposal plant? You may feel like you need to get listings at all costs, but once in a while a listing just isn't worth the trouble.

ESTATE SALES

It may seem a bit ghoulish, but when people die or go into long-term care, someone has to sell their houses. It's *very* important to be tactful if you try this approach, since it can easily offend people if done gracelessly. If someone has just died, don't approach bereaved relatives; talk to the attorney or executor of the will, or the guardian or home administrator if someone is in a long-term care facility. If you're naturally bubbly and upbeat as a sales agent, tone it down when talking to people who are close to the recently deceased or institutionalized.

Terry Kulka, a real estate sales associate in Oakland, California, followed probate listings when she first started in real estate. "I followed up estates in probate that I read about in a local legal newspaper. If anybody in my area had a house on the list, I would contact the attorney, and that wound up giving me a nice base of attorney referrals over the years. Another idea is to go to convalescent, nursing, or retirement homes in the area and establish a relationship with the intake person there, someone who is a resource to talk to people who are maybe thinking of selling their homes." Members of the clergy may also be resources. If you have friends who work or volunteer in a nursing home or hospice, they may be able to put you into contact with the appropriate administrator, and they may also be sources of information and referrals.

FLOOR TIME AT AN AGENCY

If you're part of a real estate agency, you may be able to spend a certain amount of time working the floor and phone lines at that agency. (How this works varies from agency to agency.) As Pat Farthing, broker associate of Coldwell Banker George T. Decker, in Binghamton, New York, says, "After new agents are trained in our agency, they're allowed to sign up for floor-time shifts. Each day for three-hour periods, the offices have an agent available to answer the phone. Any calls that come in that are not directed to a particular agent are transferred to the floor-time agent on duty. This agent can field the calls, which may lead to potential customers. Sometimes people walk in, as well, and they are referred to the floor-time agent. When working floor time, dress as if you're expecting to meet with a client—professionally yet comfortably, but not too casually."

FOR SALE BY OWNERS (FSBOS)

Sometimes it pays to talk to people who have been trying to sell a property by themselves. Most people have no idea of the amount of work that's involved in selling a house. Very few owners will spend the time and money it takes to promote their property effectively—and many of them don't know how to advertise properly. If sellers have been trying to move a property for a few weeks with little success, you may be able to convince them that it's easier and more cost effective in the long run to sell their property through you.

LOCAL RESOURCES

Find the people in your neighborhood who always know what's going on and talk to them. Are you friends with the clerks at the post office? Postal clerks always know who's moving. Similarly, landscape professionals, carpenters, and painters are usually tied into local information networks and know who's thinking of moving or trading up. The person who mows your lawn may prove to be a valuable resource—he or she knows the neighborhood inside and out and is aware of any changes as soon as they happen. Carpenters and painters talk to each other at the hardware store and often know who's interested in having a house built or updated—and who's thinking about selling the house they're in now, once the renovation in complete.

UNIVERSITY HOUSING OFFICES

Even if you don't handle rentals or want to deal with college students, you should make friends with people in any local college or university housing offices. Faculty members and administrators are usually hired from outside of the local area (often after national searches), and the human resources department will refer any questions they have about where to live to the housing office. Most housing offices have a list of real estate agents that they give out to newly hired faculty and administrators, and they may even recommend particular agents. Make sure that you get on that list of preferred agents.

It's a good idea to give the housing office a supply of your cards or flyers, along with any freebies, such as pens and memo pads, to give to prospective buyers, and so they see your name often. (See page 56-60)

Some large corporations have housing offices, as well, or their human resources departments may refer employees who are relocating to particular real estate agents. You will want to call and find out the procedure to get on the lists for various companies. Give them flyers and other freebies, too.

REFERRALS

Referral customers are just about always better than customers you get through cold calls, open houses, or walk-ins. For one thing, referrals know somebody who is satisfied with the quality of your work. You don't have to worry about gaining their trust—you just have to avoid losing it.

As mentioned, most of your initial referrals will come from friends and family and from their circles of friends and relatives. As you gain more experience, more of your referrals will begin to come from other sources, especially successful buyers. (You won't get as many referrals from successful sellers since many of them are moving out of the area.) Once you've been in the business for a few years, about half of your performance will be based on referrals.

Don't take referrals for granted, however. Be sure to thank friends or relatives who send customers your way, even if the referrals don't pan out. If people who are referred to you aren't in the market for or decide not to buy a house but you're on friendly terms, stay in touch with them occasionally. Sometimes a referral that doesn't work out one year will turn into a sale the next. Or referrals that ended up with another agent will later wish they had chosen you and will send friends and relatives your way. The point is, you never know. Never burn bridges and always act professionally.

COMPETING FOR LISTINGS

Sometimes you're not the only agent to whom potential sellers are talking. Many sellers will interview several agents before settling on a listing agent. They may pick agents that they like or have some contact with (such as an agent who called or left a flyer in the past), agents who were referred to them by friends or relatives, or agents whose ads they liked in the paper. You may find yourself competing not only with other agents but with a seller's preconceptions about who you are as well. A client who comes to you through a referral probably knows something about you, but clients who come to you through ads or walk-ups may have picked you out for more arbitrary (or even completely random) reasons.

To stand out at that interview, it's important to be both professional and personal. No one is going to trust you with their house unless they're convinced that you can sell it, and as a new agent, you can't fall back on a long track record to convince clients of your expertise. Make sure that you're well prepared. Be on time, don't keep the sellers waiting, and know your facts—and the key details of the sellers' neighborhood—by the time you sit down with potential clients.

But none of that will do you any good if you can't connect emotionally with the sellers. Listen closely to what the sellers tell you about their needs and their goals. Try not to make snap judgments based on first impressions, and don't stop listening because you're trying to concentrate on what you're planning to say next. Once the sellers have eliminated anyone they don't trust or who they feel isn't capable of selling the house, they're going to pick the real estate agent who they feel most comfortable with—the one they feel is most likely to address their needs and concerns while selling their house. In short, they're going to pick the best listener.

PREPARING SELLERS

Once you have a listing signed up, you need to prepare those clients to actually sell their home. By the time clients sign up for a listing, you'll need to have done your homework. You should know the clients' neighborhood, including all its features, drawbacks, and quirks. In addition, you should have looked up comparable houses that have sold recently and are active at the moment, so you can advise your clients on setting a sale price for their home. Before you walk through a house with your clients, you'll want them to be comfortable with you, and you'll want to feel comfortable knowing that you understand the house in the context of its surroundings—so you can do as good a job as possible setting it up for sale.

INITIAL LISTING APPOINTMENT

When you first sit down with potential sellers to talk about listing their home, make certain you explain the whole process to them. The more clients know what to expect from the beginning, the fewer problems and misunderstandings there will be later. Take your time with the listing and address all of your potential clients' concerns. Back up any points you make with evidence, drawn from other houses that are for sale or have recently sold in the sellers' neighborhood. A three-hour initial appointment is not unusual, given how many topics are touched on and how big a decision selling a house is for most people.

Make sure that the clients know that selling a house is a team effort— it's not just a matter of signing a paper and letting the real estate sales agent handle it. Sellers will need to do their part in preparing the house, and time spent at the initial meeting explaining how their participation can improve the eventual selling price is likely to help the process along. An agent who tries to get the listing too quickly without explaining everything to the sellers and making certain they are is comfortable is asking for trouble or misunderstandings later in the sales process. The initial meeting gives you a chance both to educate your clients and to establish a relationship.

Some other things you'll talk about at the first meeting:

✓ **Pricing**—Even if the sellers don't make a final decision at this point, this is where you give them the information they need to make an informed decision. You can lay out a price range, show how much similar properties have sold for (and how long they took to sell), and explain where your figures come from. Always substantiate everything with documentation.

✓ **Advertising**—In how many publications do you advertise the home, and what sort of response can the seller expect from those advertisements? Are you a member of a particular real estate board? How many real estate agents will have access to the listing, and how many potential buyers looking at the house does that typically translate to for a house comparable to theirs?

✓ **Showing**—Lay the groundwork for any changes you may ask the clients to make after you look at their house. Emphasize what it will take to showcase the house's strengths. (See pages 45–47 for more on this.)

✓ **Your own abilities**—What's your track record and what are your strengths as an agent? What kind of communication should the sellers expect?

EMOTIONAL ATTACHMENTS

Remember that just about all sellers are emotionally attached to their homes, no matter what they say. Be careful not to trample on homeowners' feelings or memories by sounding too callous or commercial about the home in which they may have grown up, or lived for years, or raised a family. The wrong word can turn an already emotionally distraught client into a difficult person to deal with, especially in cases of sales following a death or divorce.

You may want to try to use the owners' attachments as a selling tool. Find out what the owners think is special about the house. Was it a wonderful place to grow up because of all the kid-size nooks and crannies and the great climbing trees in the back? Try to communicate these features to potential buyers; furthermore, sellers will be happier that you are trying to sell the property to someone who appreciates it for the same reasons they do. Getting the sellers' input in this way makes them active and willing participants in the sale and it also helps prevent them from balking later if they feel that potential buyers don't respect whatever it is that they love about the house.

Pay attention to what the sellers tell you, and act appropriately. If the sellers are moving to a larger house, it's fine to talk about how wonderful the family touches in their present house are. However, if the sellers are getting divorced and the property is being sold as part of a settlement, you'll want to avoid anything that's likely to stir up already volatile emotions and memories.

DECIDING ON A SELLING PRICE

In most cases, a selling price range is pretty easy to determine once you've established some comparable properties that have sold recently or are on the market now (often three of each is a good figure to aim for). But there are still some factors to think about before recommending a price to clients.

✓ Is your client under pressure to sell in a hurry? Is there a foreclosure looming, or are there other financial problems? You may want to price the house at the low end of the range—maybe $10,000 below the normal asking price—for a quick sale. If you're in a fast-moving market or the foreclosure is still a few months off, you may want to start a property at a normal price and then lower the price if it doesn't sell in a month.

✓ Some clients are under no pressure to sell at all and are determined to get top dollar, even if it takes years. If you like the listing and are confident that the house will sell eventually, you may want to price at the high end of the range. But unless you're in a very fast-moving market, be prepared to spend a long time (and a fair amount of advertising money) earning that higher-than-usual commission. Every experienced agent seems to have a story about a difficult-to-sell house that he or she eventually got the full asking price for—after two or three years of trying.

The final choice of price is up to the sellers, but the more you explain about how houses are priced, the more likely they are to price their house at an appropriate level. Many real estate agents bring pictures of comparable houses and explain how each one is similar and different from the sellers' property and why each one sold for the price it did.

COACHING SELLERS IN WHAT TO EXPECT

Before you begin showing a house, you need to thoroughly prepare the sellers for the sale. They need to know what to clean, what to paint, what to fix—and what to expect emotionally. They need to be warned about the questions buyers will ask (if they'll be home when people are looking at the house). They need to know what to do with their pets and/or children while the house is being shown. They need to know any other details that will have to be taken care of for a sale to succeed.

One problem is that over time, people's possessions and habits become invisible to them. Because the owners have spent time in the living room for so many years, the ugly, faded wallpaper and the stained shag carpeting that buyers shudder at go unnoticed by the owners. Sometimes clients will be reluctant to change things that seem like obvious problems; therefore you will need to be extraordinarily tactful. You will also need to know what will really hurt a sale and have the biggest impact on buyers.

Some things you will have to insist on. You must tell clients to keep the front of the house immaculate. People judge a house by the entrance. If the entrance is not neat, buyers expect other problems inside. If the house is tobacco permeated or filled with pet odors, those odors will need to be taken care of, as well. Be careful not to go the other way—a house that smells too strongly of cleaning solvents and air freshener will come off as a house that has something to hide.

A few examples of how to present problems:

WHAT TO CHANGE	HOW TO EXPLAIN IT TO CLIENTS
Limit the number of personal touches in the home. This may mean taking down some decorations or heirlooms.	"Too many personal touches remind potential buyers that it's someone else's house. You want buyers to walk through and visualize how this would feel as *their* house."
Replace old or hard-to-use faucets and other fixtures.	"You don't want to make buyers think that the bathrooms are inconvenient or hard to use. You may know that everything's fine and easy to fix, but a buyer might not realize it."
Get rid of clutter.	"We want to show buyers how much space there is in the house." Also, "It will be easier for you to pack and move later if you have a yard sale now."

Make sure the house is immaculate.

"You want to remind buyers of what the house will look like when they move in. If there aren't any distractions, they can visualize the house as *theirs*." Encourage the sellers to have professional cleaners in for a thorough job, which will keep them from having to do the really unpleasant parts of cleaning.

Add a fresh coat of paint to dingy or odd-colored rooms.

"Neutral colors allow buyers to visualize how they would use a room and get them in more of a buying mood." Emphasize that the current appearance of a room might limit a buyer's imagination.

Make minor repairs, especially to the front of the house and the first rooms people see.

"You don't want anything to distract buyers from special features and character of a home."

Make sure the yard is well maintained and recently mowed.

"You want the yard to look easy to maintain." Also, "You want to emphasize how nice it is to walk around the yard." A neatly kept yard will also minimize any allergy problems buyers might have.

Get large pets out of the way.

"Some people are really afraid of big dogs, and they won't come in if they see the dog." Also, "You want to be sure your pet isn't spooked by all the confusion." If the owners can take the dog for a long walk while the house is being shown, it gets them out of the way, as well.

Minimize the impact of kids.

"Sometimes people are uncomfortable around kids." Also, "People will be so busy paying attention to your kids that they won't be able to look at the house." Minimize the impact of children on the house. If possible, have the sellers take the kids out while potential buyers are looking at the house, since you don't know how kids will react to strangers wandering through their home.

Work out an approach to selling each client's property right away. The more direction, guidance, and reassurance you can give sellers up front, the more likely they are to listen to your advice—and the more likely their property is to sell quickly. Always be reassuring and tactful when making any suggestions, and don't ever sound as if you are judging your clients. It's their house, and it's none of your business how they live in it most of the time; make it clear that you're just making suggestions for the best way to show their property off to potential buyers (and to highlight the things that buyers would notice), which is very different from how a house looks when it's actually being lived in and used normally.

PREPARING SELLERS

You have to prepare sellers little by little. You can't throw everything at them at once. In my office we have a booklet for sellers. It's very hard to tell somebody who's lived in a house for twenty years and thrown their laundry under the bed for that whole time that they can't

throw their laundry under the bed anymore. That's an
extreme example, but if I have a listing and I know those
people leave their dishes in the sink, before the house is
shown I'll run over there first to make sure that there are
no dishes in the sink. Successful REALTORS take care
of these details.

—ROBERTA DINERSTEIN, Broker, Arvida Realty
Services, Boca Raton, Florida

SOME OTHER THINGS TO REMEMBER IN
PREPARING A HOUSE

Let sellers know that not everyone is going to spend a lot of time looking
at the house. Features that are important to the sellers may not make much
of an impression on potential buyers. And potential buyers are often out-
spoken when it comes to features that they don't care for. Worse, many of
these people cannot visualize a beautiful room beneath its current decor,
and they are liable to comment cruelly on the owners taste in window
treatments, carpeting, or collectibles.

Suggest firmly that the sellers avoid being at home when the house is
shown. Sometimes it's unavoidable, but it's hard for buyers to visualize the
house as their own if the current owners are watching their every move.

If the sellers are building a new house, they need to be aware of other
potential problems. Remind them that they're unlikely to get the old house
sold and the new house built all at the same time. They need to have a
backup plan and a backup place to stay so if a buyer walks into this property and wants it in two to four weeks, they are prepared to move out within a month.

Ralph Tamper advises a direct approach to preparing clients: "You need
to make certain that they get the house ready for showing and fix those little things, or let them know that it is going to cost them dearly in the price
they can expect for their house. You need to be straightforward with them
and tell them what they need to do to get the place ready to show well.

Many agents are kind of timid about this, but being timid isn't going to sell houses."

NEGOTIATING POINTS FOR SELLERS

When you walk through the house, you'll want to start thinking about selling points. What are the best features of the house? Have special updates been made recently? Are the owners offering any other special incentives that buyers will find enticing (such as owner financing)? Pat and Ed Farthing suggest paying attention to the following possible negotiating opportunities:

- ✓ **Appliances**—Are the appliances new? Have any of them been replaced recently? Is there anything special about the appliances (such as a Subzero refrigerator or a commercial stove)?

- ✓ **Energy audit**—Is the house particularly energy efficient? Have there been updates to the insulation or the windows?

- ✓ **Roof**—Is the roof recent? Does it have any special features (like expensive cedar shingles or slate)?

- ✓ **Bathrooms**—Are there special features, like a spa or Jacuzzi? If not, is the plumbing laid out in a way that a prospective buyer could easily update it?

- ✓ **Heat and hot water**—Is the furnace or boiler new? Is it particularly high capacity, or especially fuel-efficient?

- ✓ **Storage**—Are there a lot of closets? How big are they?

- ✓ **Garage**—If there is a garage, how big is it? Does it have electricity or other modernizations? Is it easily convertible to other uses?

- ✓ **Attic and basement**—Are they finished or unfinished? Does the space suggest a lot of potential uses that buyers might be attracted to?

- ✓ **Utilities and sewer**—If the house has public utilities, how good are they? Are they comparatively inexpensive? If it has well water and a septic system, how recently have they been updated or checked? How does the water taste?

✓ **Light**—What's the light like in the house? Do certain rooms get a lot of light? Are there great views from particular rooms that you will want to make certain buyers see?

Every house has some special feature, something that can be turned into a positive note that makes it stand out from other houses. What are the features that make the house distinctive? Think about the best ways to highlight those features to clients. A house adjoining an old graveyard doesn't have to be creepy—you can emphasize its connection with local history and its quiet, peaceful character.

UNREALISTIC EXPECTATIONS

Many sellers have unrealistic expectations regarding how quickly their house will sell or, more commonly, how much money they can get for it. While you can educate sellers and try to temper their expectations, they won't always listen. Sometimes only the experience of having a house go a month or two with no serious interest will convince them.

After all, while sellers can decide on the asking price for a property, the sales price is determined by the buyers. If a house is overpriced either no one looks at it, or the wrong people look at it.

Here's an example offered by an expert broker, "If you have a house that's priced at $300,000 and should be $250,000, you may have $300,000 buyers looking at it. They don't want it—they want a $300,000 house. The wrong people are looking at the house and therefore, no one makes an offer." Especially with the spread of buyer brokerage, home buyers—even first-time buyers—tend to be very well informed. Unless the market is very tight, the house has extraordinary features, or the sellers are really lucky, buyers are unlikely to overpay for a house. Most often, an overpriced house will just sit until the sellers adjust their price to reflect market conditions.

WHEN A LISTING IS NOT WORTH THE TROUBLE

Sometimes a listing just isn't worth it. When you're starting out, you don't want to turn down any potential listing, but now and again someone will ask you to do the impossible. If a property is grossly overpriced for its condition or location, or if it has other huge problems that the owners seem unable or unwilling to do anything about, sometimes you just have to politely decline the listing.

Think about turning down a listing if:

✓ The sellers are abusive or abrasive, or seem impossible to work with for other reasons (e.g., some sellers have gender, race, or ethnicity issues).

✓ The sellers seem impossible to satisfy or demand huge rebates or givebacks in return for the sale.

✓ The sellers have no compelling reason to sell the house (if they insist on an outrageous price and don't care how long it takes the house to sell). As one agent puts it, "It's a nice dream, but it's not going to happen."

Declining a listing is pretty rare. For most agents it happens maybe once or twice a year, if that. If you find yourself turning down listings much more often, the problem may be with you. (You may want to refer back to the communication skills section of Chapter 2.)

SUMMING UP

Referrals are the best way to get listings from sellers, but you can try other techniques if you're unable to get enough referrals.

To have a successful listing, you need to build a relationship with the sellers. If possible, you want to make them feel like active participants in the selling process. Expect sellers to be emotionally involved in the sale of their homes, regardless of what they say.

Most houses will need a lot of cleaning and preparation before they're ready to show and you should expect to play an active role in preparing the house. It's up to you to explain to sellers what's needed to best show off their property and to enlist them into actively participating in the sale process.

ALL ABOUT BUYERS

- How does a new agent find buyers and turn them into listings?

- How do you turn unrealistic expectations into a helpful real estate partnership?

Finding and preparing buyers is a little easier than finding and preparing sellers. For one thing, buyers are more likely to come looking for you, particularly once you start to establish listings. Potential buyers will see your listings or advertisements and come to you. Then, it's a matter of figuring out what the buyers can afford and finding them a property that fits their needs.

Once a buyer approaches you, the process is a lot less time-consuming than with sellers: Buyers can be prequalified or preapproved quickly (sometimes in a matter of minutes), and looking at houses the same day.

While buyers, like sellers, often have unrealistic expectations, and problem buyers can be just as frustrating as problem sellers, most buyer problems can be settled quickly and up-front—or if the problems are bigger, buyers can be politely turned away before a buyer brokerage agreement is signed.

One of the first things to keep in mind when you're looking for buyers is not to ignore potential clients because of your own preconceptions. In the same way you need to educate buyers and sellers about their unrealistic expectations, you'll need to guard against making the same kind of mistake yourself.

AVOID PREJUDGING CLIENTS

Be very careful not to make judgments about potential buyers based on their appearance. Wait for the banker to tell you how much a buyer can afford to spend before you make any decisions about someone's economic level or buying power. The couple looking at houses in jeans and old boots over the weekend may spend their workweek in power suits—or may own their own dot.com empire.

REALTOR® Gayle Dinerstein had a customer who owned two Mercedes but went to look at houses in a beat-up station wagon and wearing a running suit. The listing agent for one house she showed him was reluctant to let the buyer in the door because of his appearance. Agent Louise Barbee, of American Heritage in Nashville, Tennessee, relates the frequently repeated anecdote of the young, naive-sounding man in sweat pants who was neglected by several real estate agents who never realized he was a professional football player.

In the early 1970s, one of our experts was starting out as an independent broker, an African American couple came to an open house posing as potential buyers. It turned out that they were working for an antidiscrimination group, trying to catch agents in an act of discrimination. However, they were treated fairly, and they went on to tell the broker what they were up to. He relates, "Incidents like these prove time and again that you never know who your potential customer is, how much he can afford, or what kind of taste he's going to have. You can't judge the person by the clothes he wears, especially with today's casual business dress codes. Take the executive that's got a suit and tie on all day long. He may be the world's most enthusiastic outdoorsman, and when he gets home from work he's heading out for some fishing or going down to the driving range. He's wearing jeans and dirty boots, or some wornout sweatpants, and if he's driving by an open house, he's going to pop in. And remember, sometimes people are checking *you* out. They're not coming to the open house as a buyer; they're thinking of putting their home on the market and they want to see how you're going to handle customers. You never know. Be mindful of maintaining a professional and hospitable demeanor, and you'll always do the right thing."

SOME TECHNIQUES FOR FINDING BUYERS

- **Cards and flyers**—The things many people remember you by. You'll want to get your cards and flyers into as many hands as possible; even people who aren't buying a house now may remember you down the road.
- **Freebies**—Give away eye-catching and useful items (like notepads, pencils, or Frisbees). People remember your name every time they use something you've given them.
- **Open houses**—Open a house up for prospective buyers to walk through on a given day. Potential buyers can walk through even if they don't have appointments or prequalification; many people begin looking for a house this way before deciding on an agent.
- **Farming**—a neighborhood Make certain anyone who is buying or selling a house in a neighborhood knows who you are.
- **Local media**—Small media outlets are often starving for content and will print anything you send them, which amounts to free advertising.
- **Organizations**—The groups you belong to and hobbies you participate in are a constant source of potential buyers.
- **Sponsorships**—Helping community organizations can give you visibility while emphasizing your ties to the area.
- **New homes**—Working with new construction can be a good, low-pressure way for a new real estate agent to make sales.

- **Relocations**—People who are moving to an area for new jobs or job transfers need someone to help them find housing.
- **Advertising**—The most common way for people who are not referrals to find out about you is to see the way you advertise your listings—and yourself.
- **Referrals**—It's still the best way to find clients; people who are sent your way by family, friends, or satisfied customers are your most solid client base.

FINDING BUYERS

You'll find buyers in some of the same ways you find sellers; Open houses (you can assist at other real estate agents' open houses at first and hold your own, once you're better established), farming a neighborhood, advertising, memberships in organizations (such as Rotary Club, the gym, or a church club), and floor time are all possible sources of buyers. Once again, however, your circle of friends and relatives—and their friends and relatives—will be your best source of clients. As with sellers, there is no better client than a referral.

CARDS AND FLYERS

In addition to always having business cards available (with daytime, home, and cell phone or beeper number so you can be reached at all times), you will want to have flyers made up that describe you and your strengths as a real estate agent. You will want to address why people should work with you? What do you want a stranger's first impression of you to be? Some things you might put in a flyer include:

✓ **Brief (one-paragraph) biography**—Highlight your skills, accomplishments, and community ties.

✓ **Picture of yourself**—Have it taken by a professional; it's the first impression many people will get of you, and you want it to be an accurate reflection.

✓ **Pictures of some of the types of houses you most like to sell**—Include either your listings, houses you have sold, or other agents' houses that you would like to sell.

✓ **Professional affiliations and memberships**—Listing these will help establish that you are both professional and proactive.

✓ **Phone numbers and complete contact information**—People might take both a card and a flyer, but chances are they'll lose one or the other.

If you're not up to designing a flyer yourself, many inexpensive programs, such as Microsoft Publisher, have templates that can be filled in easily with very little practice. Or, just about any printer can design a flyer for a nominal fee as part of your order. Just be certain you have all the information you need (including artwork) before you go to the printer. The same is true for cards, assuming you're not with an agency that has a uniform design.

SOME FLYER DESIGN GUIDELINES

- A little bit goes a long way—don't overdesign.
- Limit yourself to two or three fonts—one font for text and no more than two display fonts for headlines and titles.
- Use an easy-to-read text font such as Times, Courier, Palatino, Garamond, or Bookman. Do not use script fonts for normal text.
- The display fonts should fit with your text font and with each other—don't use fonts that are too unlike each other, like heavy block type together with a delicate script font.

    ◆ Leave some white space, and don't try to crowd too much into your flyer. If there's no open space or the type is too small, the flyer will be hard to read.

Printing prices vary dramatically from business to business, so get several quotes. You may want to ask other real estate agents you work with where they had flyers done (assuming you like the quality of the work). Here are some helpful tips:

✓ Make sure the price is for flyers that have already been folded—you don't want to be folding 1,000 flyers by hand.

✓ One-color trifold flyers are cheap but not very impressive. Two-color trifold flyers on glossy paper are a nice compromise. They're not too expensive (about 20 to 30 cents apiece in bulk) and they look good. Four-color flyers look the best, but are two or three times more expensive. You'll need four colors if you want color photos in your flyer, but you may not want to spend the money if the flyer is mostly text about you, rather than about the pictures.

✓ *It's very important that you check spelling and grammar* on the text for your flyer before you have it printed. If you're not the best writer in the world or can't find the words to put your strengths down on paper, find someone who can do the job. This is an area where it's worth spending the money to go to a professional. Your flyers are the first thing many potential clients will see about you. If they think you didn't bother to take the time to proofread your spelling, they won't trust you to not make the same kind of sloppy mistakes in other real estate paperwork—mistakes that will cost them money.

THE INTERNET

More and more people have begun using the Web as their first stop for information—and that includes information about real estate. You'll want to be sure that your name comes up when people search for information about real estate in your area. That means you'll need a clear, well organized Web page that doesn't take too long to load. Your page should be linked to any local real estate sites, as well as to the local chamber of commerce or other local area sites that allow commercial links.

The index to your homepage should list your name, your agency, the names of the towns and neighborhoods you work in, and other key words such as "realty" and "real estate." Your page should also have a title that's likely to come up if people do a Web search for houses in your area. For more information on setting up websites, see page 146.

One thing to avoid is commercial list of names offered over the Internet. Some services offer to sell you names and e-mail addresses of people in your area so you can farm a neighborhood via e-mail, supposedly saving yourself time and money. Avoid the temptation. Many people will consider this sort of unsolicited e-mail annoying. At best, most of your messages will be deleted unread (unlike flyers, which people do look at). At worst, you may get complaints to your Internet service provider (ISP) and have your account terminated. The Internet is a terrific tool for real estate agents, but you need to exercise some judgment in how you use it. For more information on using the Internet, see Chapter 8.

FREEBIES

One way to get people familiar with your name is to give away useful items as freebies. Pick items that last a while and are relatively inexpensive yet are made of good-quality material with your name and logo imprinted (from less than $1 per piece to about $5 each). Make certain your name is imprinted in a way that people see it regularly and it won't wear off.

Tailor your giveaway items to the community you'll be giving them out in. If you work with a lot of businesspeople, then pens, pads, or Post-it® notes will get a lot of use. For an older demographic, T-shirts or sun visors might be better received. Some good choices for freebies include:

baseball caps
calendars
car sun shields
coffee mugs
desk clocks
Frisbees
keychains
mini-flashlights
notepads
paper clip dispensers
pencils (especially fancy ones with sparkles or holographic images)
pens
Post-it® notes
sun visors
T-shirts
tote bags
water bottles

OPEN HOUSES

Our experts stress the importance of open houses for new agents looking to find buyers. "In our area, there are tons of open houses. If an agent can develop a rapport with new buyers, the agent can usually pick them up as potential buyers." Open houses give new agents a chance to meet potential buyers in an environment where the focus is on the house rather than on how smooth or experienced-sounding you are. If buyers like the way you handle yourself and feel comfortable with you, it will be an important factor in their decision to work with you.

If you don't have any listings of your own, see if you can help out a more experienced agent who doesn't have time to be at an open house for one of his or her listings. Keep a book for people to sign in and leave their names and addresses, so you can contact them later. (Encourage people to sign in, but don't be too forceful about it; it's not worth losing potential clients over formalities.) Give everyone your flyer, and have material describing the house available to give anyone who wants it.

Often agents prepare a one-page "fact sheet" on the house for prospective buyers and browsers alike to take with them. Some things to remember on fact sheets:

- ✓ Make certain that all the spelling and grammar is correct.

- ✓ Ensure that the text reads easily and avoid jargon.

- ✓ Provide all the basic information on the house—size; number of rooms; age; recent updates; sewer, water, and utility information; amount of land, outbuildings, etc.

- ✓ Present comparable information on similar homes in the same area.

- ✓ Mention any special historical details—Did Washington sleep here? Was it on a key Civil War marching ground? Is it an early example of a particular architectural style?

- ✓ Use a good-quality photocopier so the fact sheets look crisp.

- ✓ If you use colored paper, don't pick a color that clashes with the points you're making—for example, don't use a neon color for a stately colonial house.

FARMING A NEIGHBORHOOD

The idea of farming a neighborhood is to build name recognition and make certain people in a particular area think of you when they decide to contact an agent about buying a house. Even if most people aren't home during the day, you can still leave a flyer, and if people come home—especially in a subdivision, or a semipopulated area—and they find a flyer on the door, this very clearly indicates an aggressive, hardworking, very thorough person. You choose a neighborhood that you'd like to do business in, and saturate it, let them know you know the area.

This is an ideal strategy for new agents, because it sidesteps the issue of experience—the first thing potential clients encounter is not you but your carefully worded flyer. Even if you don't have any listings, you can drop off a flyer that lets people know who you are and shows them some of the houses for sale in their area (even if they're not your listings). If people are thinking of moving or upgrading their house, or if they have a friend or coworker who's looking for a house, they'll know who you are. As Farthing says, "You can build awareness and a presence for yourself. You can start with nothing. The problem today is reaching people. We're all busy, we're all running around. This way, when it's printed matter left at the door, someone can read it at his leisure, and it has a lot of impact. And, it says a lot for the agent putting forth the effort."

WHERE TO LEAVE FLYERS

Make certain to leave flyers or cards on community bulletin boards, at supermarkets, at yard sales, and anywhere else where people will notice them. Don't forget bulletin boards of organizations or clubs you belong to, or places you regularly frequent, such as the gym, tennis club, or bowling alley. Your spouse or friends may have bulletin boards at work. In rural areas, many restaurants and food stands have bulletin boards. Just be careful not to leave flyers or cards where they will offend people. In addition, be sure to confirm with whoever is in charge that it's okay to leave your materials. Restaurants, yes. Funeral homes, no. (See Chapter 2 for a detailed list of ideas.)

LOCAL MEDIA

If you're a good writer, community and weekly newspapers are almost always looking for people to write columns. A short article on some real estate topic of local interest will provide you with a lot more exposure than most ads. People will remember your name in the byline and perceive you to be an expert in the field. Plus, the staff at the newspaper are likely to recommend you to people.

The same thing is true of many radio stations, especially in smaller markets, where talk radio hosts often have to scramble to fill guest slots. If you're articulate on the air and comfortable answering callers' questions, many radio stations will be happy to have you as an occasional guest.

ORGANIZATIONS

As with finding sellers, the organizations you belong to and the hobbies or charities you participate in are good sources of potential buyers. While fellow organization members are not quite as good as referrals from friends, family, or previous customers (they don't have a reason to trust you when they first meet you), you know that you have a common interest and some shared ground with them. And, other more experienced organization members can also be great resources for help and information.

Make sure to stay active and be reliable in the organizations you belong to. If you promise to bake cookies, chair a fund raiser, or help a fellow member train for a marathon, you need to be there. You may not have been in the real estate business long enough to build up a reputation for reliability, but you can build that reputation in the community groups you participate in. And if you have a reputation for not showing up at meetings or not keeping your word, people are not going to trust you to help them buy a house—one of the biggest and most important events in most people's lives.

SPONSORSHIPS

Another way to build your reputation as an important part of the community is through sponsorships. (If you're part of an agency, you may already help sponsor some organizations.) Many community groups are looking for financial help and will promote your name in return. Whether it's buying an ad in the high school graduation program or contributing a trophy for the local martial arts club's tournament, there are many ways you can help sponsor a group—and most of them are fairly inexpensive. Some groups that may need sponsors are:

animal shelters
bands—both school and community
bowling leagues
community dance programs
community theater programs
graduation programs
Little League teams
Football leagues
public basketball leagues—youth and adult
public league soccer teams—youth and adult
school honor societies
school newspapers
school play programs
school yearbooks
Scout groups

New Homes

New homes can be a good way for agents who aren't sure of themselves to start out. There's a big difference between selling new homes and being involved in all types of real estate. Those who sell new homes at first are probably hired by a management firm to represent the development exclusively. The firm places agents at a site, and no matter what the price, people come in and talk in direct response to the advertisement. You don't have to go looking for the people. Another point to remember is that people who are building new homes are frequently also selling their current homes. In addition to picking up potential buyers, you may be able to acquire a property listing.

Relocations

Get to know the personnel officers at major corporations with branches in your area. When people are hired from out of state or transferred to the area, often the personnel office refers them to a local real estate agent or gives them a list of agents to choose from. If you have a reputation in the office of being easy to work with and understand the corporate culture of the company, you stand a good chance of being that agent. The better you know the area—what neighborhoods have the best schools, in which areas will a newly relocated executive and his or her family feel most comfortable—the more successful you will be. And a company executive who is happy with your work may be a powerful promoter and source of referrals for years to come.

If you have any freebies that are useful in an office environment, such as calendars, notepads, or Post-it® notes, make certain to give some to local personnel officers.

ADVERTISING

If you're with an agency, you will probably be incorporated into the general agency advertising strategy. You still should make certain your listings are focused, accurate, and hard hitting. (see Appendices A and B.) In general, always keep an eye out for advertising opportunities that reach as many potential buyers as possible without being outrageously expensive. In addition to local real estate flyers and magazines and newspapers, be on the alert for other ad venues. A few ideas you may want to think about:

✓ **Place mats**—Many family restaurants offer business card–size advertising on place mats.

✓ **Toll booths**—Some states allow businesses that help beautify toll plazas to place small ads that are visible to thousands of motorists every day (e. g., "flowers donated by [name] Real Estate").

✓ **Mass transit**—Train and subway ads vary dramatically in price depending on the local market. Keep an eye out for bargains.

REFERRALS

Still, the best source of buyers is to remind friends, relatives, and fellow members of any organizations you belong to that you're an active real estate agent looking for clients. Make sure that you're the one they think of when they need someone to answer a real estate question. Be free with advice and assistance when people ask. It may be inconvenient now, but people will remember your ready expertise and helpfulness when they're planning to buy a house—or when someone they know is. Think of every place you go and everyone that you come in contact with as a potential customer or referral—your spouse's colleagues, parents, teachers, and coaches at your child's school or extracurricular activities, members and staff at your health club, the congregation at your place of worship, your social sphere, your sphere of influence—getting the message out that you're in real estate helps.

Referrals build on themselves. If your friends and relatives recommend you to their friends and relatives, those people will have a positive impression of you (even if they decide not to pursue a purchase at that point) and will recommend you to others, as well. If pursued effectively, recommendations build into other recommendations in a constantly expanding circle.

PREPARING BUYERS

The laws on buyer brokerage have changed dramatically over the last few years and vary quite a bit from state to state and region to region. Buyers are much more informed now, and your relationship with a home buyer is more complex than it would have been a few years ago. It's important not only that buyers sign any required disclosure forms but also that they understand those forms—and you need to be very clear on what information you're required to disclose and what information you're not allowed to disclose.

Both the buyer and seller need to understand the buyer brokerage laws. Information that is considered off limits legally or ethically will vary from area to area, so you should always check on these points with your principal broker. Be mindful of potential conflicts of interest—if you find yourself being pulled between two people you represent, your best bet may be to make sure that both parties are aware of the situation. That way you can act as a mediator rather than choosing between either the buyers' or the sellers' interests at the expense of the other party. By not keeping conflicts hidden from your clients—even if it means you spend a lot more time explaining and making sure your clients are comfortable with the situation up front—you lessen the risk of a sale being derailed because of surprise disclosures late in the deal.

Like sellers, buyers come in many types and have different needs. Don't fall into the trap of expecting buyers to fit into the same mold or into your own preconceptions. First-time home buyers may or may not have enough money to buy their dream home. Sometimes you will have to bring first-time home buyers down to earth and try to lower their expectations to get them closer to what's available in the price range the lender has told you they can afford. On the other hand, some first-time home buyers may be able to afford a mansion. Each case is different.

People who are relocating or moving up into higher-priced homes are more likely to know what to expect, since they've been through the home-buying process before. Be cautious, though—you don't want to lose a sale because you assumed the buyers understood the process better than they actually did. For all buyers, it's important that you build their trust and equally important that you stay on top of the sale process and make sure nothing falls through the cracks along the way.

CHANGING TIMES

In Connecticut, up until a few years ago, most agents were just representing sellers, and in most cases, agents looked out for the sellers' interests. As agents, we weren't dishonest with buyers, but on the other hand we were working for the sellers, and the sellers paid us. Real estate has gone through a transition. The rules have changed. Now we can represent the buyer; we can represent the seller; we can represent both parties as a dual agency; or we can be a designated agency, which is where two separate people in the office handle the case with one representing the buyer and one representing the seller.

—RUSS HICKS

THE FIRST MEETING

You want to accomplish three things in your first meeting with buyers: You want to build rapport, find out what the buyers can afford, and get a sense of what the buyers are looking for. "When a buyer comes to me, first I listen to learn about his or her desires," says agent Pat Malek. "And then I ask them a series of questions." Here are some typical questions to ask potential buyers.

- ✓ What kind of house are you looking for? Are there special features that are particularly important to you?

- ✓ Is there a particular area that you want to stay in or move to? Are there special location considerations (such as wanting to keep kids in the same school district or wanting to stay close to an aging parent)?

- ✓ What's your housing situation now? Are you in a house that you're currently selling? Are you renting a property?

- ✓ What is your time frame? Do you want to buy right away or do you have some time?

- ✓ What's your employment situation? What times are you free to look at houses? If you work at home, do you need a house zoned for mixed use?

- ✓ What is your financial picture? Have you talked to a lender? Do you know how much you can afford? Are there any special financial considerations (such as a relative providing a down payment or divorce settlement issues)?

If potential buyers have not talked with a lender yet, you can put them in touch with one on the spot. (See page 76.) The lender will do a quick prequalification and establish what price range the buyers can afford to look in. (Note that in fast-moving markets, buyers will have to be prequalified, not just preapproved.)

PREAPPROVED VS. PREQUALIFIED CUSTOMERS

Prequalified customers have met with a mortgage counselor to find out what kind of mortgage they can secure from
the lender. The mortgage counselor, or broker, takes information on income and debt load from the prospective buyers. That information is processed into a standard formula,
based on interest rates, and the customers are then qualified
for a maximum purchase price, based on normal taxes.
For preapproval, a mortgage counselor runs a credit
report and verifies income on potential buyers and quali-
fies them on maximum purchase price, contingent upon a
satisfactory appraisal of the property.

Once the buyers are prequalified, it's a good idea to jump in the car and
go look at three or four properties (preferably your own listings if any seem
to meet their needs). Show the buyers a range of houses in their price range
that have some of the characteristics they described. Looking at some
houses quickly allows you to build a rapport with the buyers and also helps
them to solidify what they're looking for. Often the kind of house buyers
have described for you in the initial meeting is very different from the
property they eventually acquire.

While most buyers have at least a hazy sense of what their dream house
looks like, they've probably got a lot of other desires for what they want in
a house, as well.

- ✓ **Size**—How much square footage are they looking for? How many
  bedrooms do they need? Do they need a lot of storage space?

- ✓ **Age**—Do they want an old house, a new one, or something in between?

- ✓ **Location**—Do they want to be in the middle of town, in the
  woods, or somewhere in between? Does the house need to be convenient to a particular highway or mass-transit line?

✓ **Style**—Are they looking for a modern ranch, a stately Victorian, a colonial with outbuildings, or something else?

✓ **History**—Do they want a historical house, or do they want to avoid the potential limitations to alterations that historic properties present?

✓ **Landscape**—Do they want something rural and wooded or an easy-to-maintain garden? How much land are they looking for?

✓ **Special features**—Do buyers absolutely have to have fireplaces, high ceilings, or other specific architectural features?

✓ **Updates**—Does the house have to have up-to-the-minute features or access to cable modem or ISDN lines? Do buyers want a house with a modern kitchen?

✓ **Amenities**—Does the property need to be close to parks, shopping, restaurants, particular specialty food stores, or a particular church or synagogue?

✓ **Neighborhood**—Are buyers looking for a particular kind of neighborhood? Are schools a consideration?

✓ **Zoning**—If the buyers work out of their home or are planning a home-based business of some sort, is the property zoned appropriately?

✓ **Cost**—Is it something they can realistically afford?

No house will fit all of these criteria. Your job is to find a house in the buyers' price range that fits as many of the criteria as possible—enough that the buyers decide it's the best house available for them. You also want to find that perfect house relatively easily, rather than having to show dozens of houses to find a match. The better your rapport with buyers, the easier time you'll have matching them with houses. If you're out of sync with your buyers, you may have to show them many houses before they're satisfied.

AGREEMENTS

It's vital to establish rapport with clients before asking them to commit to a buyer brokerage agreement (or committing yourself to their search, for that matter). While agents who represent sellers can comfortably show properties as soon as they've prequalified buyers and explained any necessary disclosure forms, buyers' agents may want to wait until they've seen a few houses with potential buyers before committing to an agreement. (In some areas, if you do not have a signed buyer brokerage agreement you may show only your own agency's listings to clients.)

Sometimes it's best to go out and look at a few houses and talk with the clients about the buyer brokerage agreement on the way back, after you've built a relationship with them and you're comfortable working with each other. Many people will be uncomfortable committing to a brokerage agreement with you before you've looked at houses together—that initial trip is the time for you to show them that you've listened to their concerns and you understand what's important to them. Once buyers feel that you really do care about their needs and aren't trying to push them toward houses they don't want, usually they will be happy to sign a buyer brokerage agreement allowing you to represent them exclusively for a set period of time, typically six months. (Specific language of buyer brokerage agreements varies from place to place.)

LISTENING TO BUYERS

The most important skill necessary to becoming a successful agent is to really listen to buyers—and that means to listen to what they mean. Most agents learn the hard way that what buyers say is not always what they mean, and they usually learn that by lost sales. I remember a buyer who told me he would only buy a house that had very specific features. He was quite definite about it. I took a chance and showed him some beautiful homes that were outside of his list features. I made sure to take note of his responses to these homes and was able to come up with some good compromises. Well, he ended up buying a house that had few of the features he was originally so adamant about, but I discovered that concentrating on his responses, and listening to what he was really saying, led to a wonderful sales experience.

—GAYLE DINERSTEIN, agent

MEETING WITH COUPLES

Once again, it's important not to make assumptions about people too quickly. If you're speaking to a couple, don't talk to just one person or another, even if one person does most of the talking. Don't assume you know who the decision maker is just because that person talks the most. Pay attention to any habits you may have unconsciously picked up. Do you tend to talk to one gender more than the other when meeting with a couple? Do you assume that one partner is dominant? Make certain you're paying attention to the couple and to what they're saying, not to your own preconceptions.

Above all, don't try to play couples against each other. If one partner disagrees with something or sounds reluctant while the other partner agrees with you, do not allow yourself to get pulled into an argument, or give in to the temptation to help the partner who agrees with you stampede the other into agreement. If they've been together long enough to buy a house together, they'll settle the fight later—but there's a good chance they'll blame you for starting it, and if they do they'll never trust you again.

SPECIAL NEEDS

Be aware of clients' physical limitations, but don't condescend to them. Generally, buyers will tell you what you need to know, but you should use common sense, as well: If the buyer is in a wheelchair or walks with a cane, a house with steep flights of stairs is probably going to present problems—as will a house with a driveway that ices up easily. Special needs might mean more than out-and-out physical disabilities. Once in a while buyers will feel uncomfortable talking about particular conditions, so you will need to be observant and tactfully ask questions when it's appropriate.

✓ Do the buyers have frail parents who visit often?

✓ Do they have asthma, hay fever, or allergies that might be worsened by living in certain areas?

✓ Do they have children with special needs?

✓ Are there disabled family members or friends who will be in the house regularly, and what's the nature of their disability?

Be aware of which houses in your area (and among your listings) are handicap accessible and which houses could be easily converted. Find out where handicap-accessible public transportation is available for disabled residents.

BUYERS' EXPECTATIONS

Often buyers come to us, and they're very confused. Many times, first-time buyers have unrealistic expectations, they think we can work miracles, like getting them their dream house, even if they have little or no money to put down. As we do our market analysis for a buyer and explain what the houses in the area of choice cost, we walk these people through a typical scenario and we very quickly cut to the chase. For example, "This house that you're talking about, the one you drove by, the pretty blue one with the picket fence, well, that's a $280,000 house, and you're going to have to have around $30,000 in cash to close it, and you're going to have a monthly payment of $2,300, and that means that you're going to have to have an income of a certain level. In other words, if you want to run this marathon, you better have good sneakers and lose about twenty pounds."

—ED FARTHING

OTHER CONSIDERATIONS

While you're first meeting with new buyers, try to get a sense of any other considerations they might have but might not think to mention. What are their hobbies? Do they like to bird watch? Do they collect motorcycles? Are they joggers? Do they have pets? Any of these interests (or a combination of them) will make some otherwise-perfect houses more or less desirable. Buyers usually will be happy to talk about their interests and, if prompted, usually will give you the information you need—after all, they want to find the perfect house to keep all their Harleys in just as much as you do.

A few other things to consider:

✓ **Noise level**—Do the buyers like peace and quiet, or are they uncomfortable in an area that isn't bustling?

✓ **Work schedule**—Is the house in an area that gets very foggy late at night when a third-shift worker will be traveling?

✓ **Neighborhood restrictions**—Historic districts or planned housing often have restrictions on colors, siding, gardens, or any visible changes home owners can make to their property. This will be a plus for some buyers and a minus for others.

✓ **Driving**—Are there steep hills or other geographical features that some buyers' vehicles won't be able to handle easily, especially in bad weather?

✓ **Hunting**—If a home is in a wooded area, is there hunting nearby during certain seasons? This may be a plus for buyers who hunt but will also restrict when it's safe to walk in the woods and what clothing is safe to wear outside during hunting season.

IF THE FIRST MEETING GOES BADLY

Sometimes buyers won't click with you or won't listen to what you're telling them. It may be worth showing them a few houses to see if things will fall into place, but occasionally you may decide that a potential buyer isn't worth the trouble. If you don't feel comfortable that you'll be able to sell someone a house, or if someone's expectations are too far out of line with reality, you may want to do both yourself and the buyer a favor and politely explain that you're not the right agent for him or her.

If buyers don't want to believe you when you explain the current market conditions, you have to decide if looking at properties will bring those buyers around to reality, or if there's a larger problem. Sometimes buyers need so much educating and handholding that it just isn't worth your time. "One of the things that new agents really need to learn," says Ralph Tamper, "is that they need to spend their time working with clients that meet their needs. There's nothing that requires an agent to work with anybody who comes through the door. You can't waste time with people who are never going to make you money."

GETTING BUYERS PREAPPROVED

In a busy real estate market, it may not be enough to get buyers preapproved—if they're not already prequalified for a loan, they may never get a chance to bid on the house they want. As Ralph Tamper puts it, "You have to have them preapproved—not just prequalified, but preapproved. For example, right now, in the greater Houston area, if you don't have preapproval, there's no way you're going to ever get near the better houses because so many people are looking at them and there's competition there for the available inventory. Talk to your buyers and get them in touch with the appropriate lenders in order to get preapproved."

In slower markets (or for buyers who are looking for less desirable properties) pre-qualification may be enough to at least make you comfortable that the buyers actually have the ability to buy the property they want.

You will get to know quickly the strengths of various lenders in your area. Ask experienced agents you work with which bankers they like to steer buyers toward. Sit down with some of the bankers you will be working with and see who you're most comfortable sending people to—and what kinds of clients they handle best. Certain banks will be better able to deal with buyers of different types. One bank may work well with self-employed buyers whom other lenders would turn away, for instance. Others may be more helpful with particular loan programs. Buyers may already have a banker in mind, but you will also want to recommend the lenders whom you feel will be the best fit for your clients.

The process of matching lenders and buyers is a sort of match-making. Some questions to keep in mind in deciding what lenders to recommend:

✓ What type of program are the buyers most suited for?

✓ Are they going to qualify for a subsidized government loan or other state or federal program?

✓ Will they be able to get a traditional loan with their current financial situation and projected down payment?

✓ If not, are they good candidates for a subprime loan at a higher interest rate (such as clients with a good income but insufficient work history in the area or not enough down payment)?

✓ Which loan officer has the programs that best fit the buyer's situation?

✓ If the client's situation is a little trickier, which loan officer has enough clout with his or her organization to get a loan approved?

Our experts describe the matchmaking process:"Every loan company or every bank will take a triple-A house and a triple-A buyer. No bank or loan organization will take a really bad house or a really bad buyer. However, most of what we're dealing with is the average intermediate buyer and intermediate house, and we have to try to match those up with a lending institution." Part of your job is to be aware of the strengths of each of the lending institutions and loan officers in your area and to be able to match them smoothly with your clients. The better you are at matching lenders to buyers, the more quickly your buyers will be approved—and the less time they will have to spend worried about financial details and money problems. You want buyers to be able to focus on visualizing the dream house you are going to help them find rather than visualizing all the paper-work they will have to do to make the sale happen.

An experienced broker like Ed Farthing usually can get buyers approved almost instantly, by having a good feel for which lender to match up with each buyer. "We can call a lender up right now, with or without the customer present, pass along the financial information and whatever price-range home they've been looking at. Within minutes we can have a fax printout of exactly every penny it's going to cost that person to fit into that program. We're not about to go spinning our wheels showing them something they can't afford. When that happens, no one wins—not you or the customer."

When the buyers have been approved (or qualified), you'll know what sort of properties you can show them. The lender will let you know what the buyers can afford and what program they will probably fit into. That may affect the houses you can show them, since certain houses may not be eligible for particular state or federal programs. For instance, most older houses are not eligible for government loans. If clients can only afford a government loan, you may have to steer them away from those houses. When you meet a prospective buyer, warn them about what types of financing are going to be required to buy the property. If they don't fit that financing, then maybe you need to move on to something else in order to save each other a lot of heartache and a lot of time.

SECONDARY LENDERS

Sometimes buyers can't qualify for a normal loan program and will arrange for a loan through a mortgage broker or other subprime lender—usually at a substantially higher interest rate than a conventional loan. Typical subprime loans carry an interest rate from one to five percentage points higher than a conventional loan and often have higher fees and closing costs, as well.

At times it makes sense to take out this sort of loan. For instance, a self-employed buyer who hasn't been in the area for long is going to have trouble getting a loan even if his or her business is booming. However, you'll want to be careful that buyers aren't getting in over their heads. A year or two in a subprime loan is fine if the buyers are going to be able to refinance quickly. It's not fine if the buyers are left with no discretionary income to deal with unexpected expenses—since unexpected expenses are a significant feature of the first few years of home ownership. Don't let buyers get in over their heads. You want them to be happy with the properties they buy through you. Your future depends on their referrals. Buyers who lose a home to foreclosure—or can't afford to go out to dinner because their mortgage payments are so crippling—aren't likely to appreciate your efforts in helping to get them into the home that ruined their lives.

NEGOTIATING POINTS FOR THE BUYER

When you're ready to start showing buyers houses, you should start thinking about the buyers' selling points. Just like the houses you list, buyers have selling points—and desirable buyers can make for a quicker sale. Think of some of the things your buyer is offering to a potential seller.

- ✓ **Preapproved mortgage**—Is your buyer in excellent financial shape? Is everything ready to close quickly as soon as an offer is accepted? Or are there factors that might delay a sale?

✓ **Timeframe**—Can your buyer move fast if the seller is in a hurry to move the property? Alternatively, if the seller needs time to vacate the property, is your buyer in a position to wait?

✓ **Repairs**—If you have a buyer who is handy and can deal with necessary small-scale repairs, he or she may be able to eliminate a huge headache for the seller.

✓ **Inspection**—Some really knowledgeable buyers will make an offer with no (or "limited") inspection. This allows for a smooth, fast sale. Be very careful about this factor, because if you have not sufficiently warned buyers about the risk of proceeding without an inspection and there turn out to be problems, you may be held partially liable. Also, check with your broker regarding local laws that govern inspection.

✓ **A nice fit**—Is this a dream home for the buyers? If the owners clearly love the home they are leaving, they may feel better about selling it to people who will value it as much as they do. Don't hesitate to pass on compliments from buyers about the style or condition of the house.

The biggest difference between success and nonsuccess is yourself. It's not about your office, it's you. You're out there selling yourself, and if you believe in yourself , if you represent yourself honestly and fairly, and if you're hard-working, it's a very simple formula for success.

—PAT MALEK

SUMMING UP

Generally, finding buyers is easier than finding sellers. Many of the same techniques work for finding both buyers and sellers, and referrals are the best way to get both.

Your first conversation with buyers should be an attempt to build rapport and get a sense of what they're looking for in a house. At the same time you should get the buyers preapproved (or, if possible, prequalified) so you know how much they can afford to spend.

Like sellers, buyers may have unrealistic expectations. The more you can explain to them up front about what to expect when house hunting, the more smoothly things are likely to go.

DURING THE SALE PROCESS

- SELLING REAL ESTATE IS LIKE AN ICEBERG—MOST OF IT HAPPENS OUT OF VIEW, LONG BEFORE OFFERS ARE MADE AND SALES ARE CLOSED.

- HOW DO YOU SHOW A HOME?

- HOW DO YOU DECIDE WHAT FEATURES TO HIGH-LIGHT TO A PARTICULAR BUYER?

- WHAT STEPS CAN YOU TAKE TO MAKE THE PROCESS OF SHOWING AND SELLING HOMES GO AS SMOOTHLY AS POSSIBLE?

The hardest part of selling houses is already done before you actually show a property to buyers. The process of finding buyers and sellers and preparing people—physically and emotionally—and their properties for sale is much more difficult and time-consuming than the rest of the sale. Once you are ready to show a property to potential buyers, you have a couple of big advantages working in your favor. Don't lose sight of your most important edge:

> The buyer wants to buy a property,
> and the seller wants to sell a property.

The rest of your job as a real estate agent is a combination of match-making (finding the right property for buyers), helping to bridge the dif-ference between what buyers expect to spend and what sellers expect to receive, and making sure all the paperwork that makes a sale official is done correctly.

By the time buyers spend money on home inspections and appraisals, you should be relatively secure that you can make the sale work—that you can keep things on track through the closing and smooth over any pitfalls along the way. That's why people hire real estate agents in the first place: The average clients buy a house maybe two or three times in their lives. They rely on you, who sells many houses a year, to give them advice and help keep them out of trouble.

This chapter is about ways to help buyers settle on a house, make a successful offer, and avoid trouble.

PREPARING TO SHOW A HOME

Preparing a home for showing and preparing to show a home are not the same thing. You'll want to consider a number of things before you show each home to potential buyers. Some of these things you can do in advance—especially when the homes are your own listings. Other decisions will have to be made on the spot when you arrive at an unfamiliar home (listed by another agent) with potential buyers in tow.

Remember to document everything that you do—every conversation and visit with your clients, both buyers and sellers. Doing this is helpful not only to avoid conflicts and misunderstandings with your clients but also for future reference. You will be able to refer to your notes for a quick refresher on the selling points of any house you have shown before, even if it's not your listing.

It's also important to call ahead and make sure the house is ready to show, even if you've confirmed the appointment previously. You don't want to spend half an hour driving clients to a potential dream house only to find that a toilet has overflowed and flooded the bathroom floor—a problem that could be cleared up in an hour but now will make the buyers question the house's plumbing and make the sale more difficult.

PICKING SELLING POINTS

What are some of the selling points to choose from? Each property you show has its own strengths and weaknesses, but don't take a "laundry list" approach to properties. Remember that each buyer has different needs, and the property that's too noisy for one buyer will be just the sort of bustling, vibrant neighborhood that another buyer is dying to live in.

Run down the following points and decide what are the best things about the property to highlight for potential buyers:

✓ **Put the best face on a house**—The front of the house makes a big first impression. What's most noticeable about the front of this property? Are there particular architectural features? Do its features make the house appear larger or smaller than it really is? Is the house especially conspicuous or inconspicuous from the street? Does the architecture make the house look distinguished? Does the property look trouble-free and easy to maintain?

✓ **The neighborhood**—What does the neighborhood have to offer? Is there any special history in the area? Does the neighborhood have a particular defining characteristic or charming feature? Is it filled with a particular type of architecture, interesting specialty shops, or other attractive features? Does it have a particular cultural heritage? Are there interesting anecdotes about people who live in the area or celebrities who grew up locally? Is there a park within walking distance? Is the house convenient to shopping?

✓ **Immediate occupancy**—Is the house ready to move into immediately? Is it empty and ready for the buyers to make it their own, or does it have a lived-in, homey feel?

✓ **Preinspected**—Has the house been inspected recently, giving buyers assurance that the property will be relatively trouble free and without hidden surprises?

✓ **Security**—Is the house in a particularly safe area? Does it have security features already installed, such as motion detectors, a burglar alarm, gates, or bars? Be careful not to present the house in such a way that it seems dangerous to live in.

✓ **Schools**—What are the public schools like? Are there private schools nearby, as well? Do any of the local schools have a particular reputation or claim to fame? For instance, is the high school band always winning awards? Is the school district near the top of the state in test scores? Is the school a football powerhouse?

✓ **Transportation**—Is the house convenient to a major highway? Is it easily accessible to an airport or rail system? Are there mass-transit options locally? Are the local roads particularly good or well maintained? Is it on one of the first roads to be plowed if there's a snowfall?

✓ **Energy efficiency**—Is the house very inexpensive to heat or cool? Low heating and cooling costs can be an important highlight at a time when oil and electrical prices are high. Does it have an energy-efficient design? Is it well insulated? Is the house cozy?

✓ **Services**—What services does the town offer? Are there good public utilities? Are there public water and sewer lines, and are the costs inexpensive? Has the fire department won statewide awards? Is the local ambulance service especially good? Is the police force well respected? Is the sanitation department a pioneer in recycling? Is the town government especially open or efficient? Is the local congressperson terrific at getting federal dollars lavished on the area?

✓ **Recreation**—Is there a beautiful park within walking distance? Does the town have a wonderful library? Are there public sports fields, jogging or bike trails, or other community-sponsored recreational facilities? Is there a good gym or health club nearby? Is the area famous for a spa or other luxury resort? Is there a state-of-the-art movie theater nearby? Are there local nightclubs? Are there local live music venues? Are there museums nearby? Is the area convenient to major sporting or concert venues?

✓ **Taxes**—Does the town have a very low mill rate? Is the property in a low-tax area compared with nearby communities? Are taxes an especially good value in the community, given the level of services? If the town has a very high tax rate, you may not want to emphasize it. If the buyer brings the point up, talk about taxes in terms of value for each tax dollar.

✓ **Environment**—Is the air quality especially good? Does the water taste good? What's the source of the town's water? Is the area renowned for the beauty of its fall foliage? Are the winters especially mild? Are the evenings cool and pleasant even on the hottest summer days?

✓ **Community activities**—What are some of the clubs and organizations that are active locally? Are there branches of the Rotary, Lions Club, or VFW in town? Are there adult sports leagues or regular bowling or golf tournaments? Are there strong churches or synagogues in the community? Is there an active community theater? Is it easy to become active in the neighborhood? Are local groups, such as the PTA and historical society, welcoming to newcomers?

✓ **Handicap Access**—Does the house have wide doorways? Is there a ramp, or space to build one easily? Are light switches and appliances easily reachable for someone in a wheelchair? Is the house especially safe for a person who's handicapped or developmentally disabled?

✓ **Tax refunds vs. renting**—Will a mortgage on this property represent a dramatic saving for the buyers at tax time? Will they end up paying less for this house than they're paying now?

✓ **Pride of ownership**—If you're working with first-time buyers, make sure they know the emotional difference between owning their own house and paying rent on someone else's property.

Always keep the buyers in mind when you're presenting these points. Remember what their desires are and that *you* are not the one buying the house. Sometimes the points that you feel are most significant won't make much difference to buyers—and you'll turn them off if you seem insensitive to their concerns. For instance, if buyers are childless by choice, they may not care how good the local school system is—and your bringing up the topic will only remind them of the high local school taxes.

Know the Route

It's important to know all the roads and byways in the area where you're selling houses. Drive around the area at different times of day, in different light, and in different seasons. Whenever you're driving in an area where you show homes, pay attention to the features around you. Obviously, you need to know the area and don't want to get lost while you're taking clients to see a house, but it's just as important to be able to pick the prettiest route to the property.

In a way, you start showing a property while you're still in a car approaching the neighborhood. The view of the area from the road is the first impression nonlocal buyers will have of the neighborhood. If the beauty of the area enchants them, they're more likely to be enchanted by the house, as well (or another one nearby). Be certain to point out any particularly beautiful features along the way or any well-known or noteworthy features of the area you're passing through.

Do a couple of other things on the trip over to the property you're showing:

✓   Make sure the clients are alert and in a house-hunting mood. Are they excited about the property, or are they preoccupied from their workday? You may want to stop for coffee or otherwise give them a chance to focus. If buyers aren't able to focus on the property, they're unlikely to see its features accurately.

✓   Talk about the house along the way. Remind clients of any special features and talk about how the house fits into what they're looking for. This is your chance to let them know what to look for in the house and to get them thinking positively about it (especially if they've looked at a lot of houses, which may all be starting to blend together in their heads). When buyers first see the house, you want their eyes to go immediately to the carved wooden door and brand-new insulated windows you've been talking about, instead of fixating on the gutters that are going to need replacing in a couple of years.

✓ If buyers are following you in their own car for some reason, be sure to give good directions. Be sure to stop at yellow lights, so you aren't separated from the buyers by a light suddenly changing after you've passed by it. You want to avoid anything that will make the buyers anxious or make them think about anything other than the house they are about to see—and, hopefully, fall in love with.

KNOW YOUR BUYERS

Always go back to your notes to refresh your memory before you meet with buyers, even if you work with them frequently. When you work with many people and see many similar properties every day, it's easy to have a momentary memory lapse or get one buyer's family situation confused with another's. But buyers can be highly offended by that meaningless lapse on your part; remember that most buyers tend to think of themselves as your only client—even if they know intellectually that you work with many other buyers.

It may seem like a lot to remember, but if you forget (since your last meeting a week ago) that a buyer's mother is sick, or that his daughter is in the state soccer final, a buyer may think of you as uncaring. And if you seem forgetful about the small details of buyers' lives, they may not trust you to remember the small details needed to help them successfully buy a house. Note the personal details that are mentioned after you drop off your prospective buyers—remembering them goes a long way when it comes to loyalty during the house-hunting process, and even further when it's referral time.

Double-check your notes for the following:

✓ **Basic information**—What kind of house are the buyers looking for? Do they want to be in a particular neighborhood? What is their dream house? How much can they afford to spend on it? Are they prequalified or preapproved for a mortgage? Whom are they considering as a lender?

✓ **Family**—How many kids do they have, and what do you know about them? Are they in the public school system? Are there other family members living with them? Do they have pets?

✓ **Special factors**—Do family members have allergies? Is there disability or long-term illness in the family?

✓ **Houses they have looked at**—What did they like and dislike? How does it compare to what they said they were looking for?

PRESENTATION STYLE

How you present a property will vary with each house and each customer. A property may have certain features that you will always highlight, but don't fall into the trap of giving a scripted-sounding description of the house. Don't just describe the house to the buyers; explain how it will fit into their lives.

You'll want both to address your clients' needs and desires and to play to your own strengths as an agent. (See page 15.) What are the things you do best when talking about or showing a house? How can you make your clients feel good about themselves in the house you are showing them? How will this house fit into their lives? Think about the following questions:

✓ What's important to your clients? What are the main concerns and desires they have expressed to you? What's really important to them in a house? Are there things they'd like to find but may have resigned themselves to not getting? How does the house you're showing them fit into their hopes and dreams?

✓ What questions do you anticipate? Are there particular areas that your clients are always concerned about? Are there issues that keep coming up when you talk to them? What are the issues they have to be satisfied with before they can settle on a house?

✓ What problems do you have to overcome? Be aware of what issues have to be settled before your clients can commit to buying a house. These issues may be emotional or financial, or in other areas. Your presentation should focus on how this house will make things better in their lives and fit in with their goals and needs for the future.

Always keep your presentation focused on how the house fits into the clients' lives; houses can't be sold in a vacuum, and even the nicest house won't sell to a buyer who can't envision living in it and making it his or her own. Choose and present your properties carefully. If you present a house and the buyers choose a different property, it shouldn't be because they feel that one was wrong but because another one was even better.

THINGS TO AVOID

Where do real estate agents go wrong in dealing with their clients? Here are some common mistakes you'll want to avoid:

✓ **Talking too much**—Describe the house as much as necessary, explain what needs to be explained, answer any questions, but don't be afraid of quiet. Let the buyers make their own decisions. Pay attention to body language; if the buyers want to walk through the house quietly before talking with you about it, let them. You want to help facilitate their purchase, not distract them from it.

✓ **Bringing up negative issues**—Don't give buyers reasons to *not* buy a house. Don't be reluctant to address negative issues if your clients bring them up, but don't bring up issues that may not have occurred to them. The exception to this is if you see something in a house that is dangerous or unsafe or will cause a house to fail inspection later (such as obvious bug damage); there's no reason to waste your clients' time on clearly unsalable houses.

✓   **Using too many buzz words**—Don't get caught up in the jargon of the profession. Explain yourself in clear, plain language. Nobody is impressed by impenetrable real estate-ese; it sounds pretentious and it will annoy your clients.

✓   **Pointing out features without revealing their benefits**—Don't assume that the buyers are thinking the same way you are or have the same knowledge you do. If you point out something as a particular feature, make sure your clients understand what's so special about it. For example, first-time home buyers might not realize how much of a comfort and cost advantage insulated windows provide if they've always rented and never had to pay heating bills.

✓   **Not listening to the wants and needs of the buyers**—Make sure you're focusing on what buyers care about in the house, not what you think is interesting. You're not the one buying the house; don't lose sight of your clients' interests and needs.

✓   **Assuming anything**—Don't get caught in the trap of taking your clients for granted or assuming you know what they're thinking and looking for. Buyers' needs evolve; as they look at more houses, your clients' thinking may change and different issues may take on greater importance. For instance, after looking at different properties, clients may decide that they don't need as much land as they thought, but the house they buy has to have extra storage space. If you don't pay attention to their changing needs and keep showing them houses with lots of acreage but no closets, you'll end up with frustrated clients—and no sale.

✓ **Rushing the buyer**—Every buyer moves at a different pace. Let your clients work at their own speed when they're looking at houses. Don't push them to meet an arbitrary schedule (and don't over-schedule clients who like to take their time in houses). It may seem strange if a potential buyer spends 20 minutes looking at a seemingly ordinary room, but you don't know what memories or ideas are going through your client's head—you might end up interrupting the buyer's memory of how much like a favorite childhood place the room is, or his or her mental plan on how to remodel it.

✓ **Making decisions for clients**—Buying a house is a stressful time for clients and a disempowering one. They have to give every financial detail of their lives to impersonal lenders, who will make seemingly arbitrary decisions on their value. Many buyers feel as if they're being treated like children. Don't reinforce that feeling by arbitrarily deciding on minor details, such as travel arrangements, without consulting the buyer first. Make sure your clients have a choice about where to meet and who drives, for instance. (Some buyers are wary of other drivers and prefer to drive in their own vehicle, even in unfamiliar areas.)

✓ **Being late**—Make a habit of always being on time or early when meeting with clients. If you're delayed by something unavoidable, be certain there's a way to call the clients so they know you're thinking about them—and don't let it happen more than once. Every buyer wants to feel as if he or she is your main priority; if you're late, buyers feel as if there's something more important to you than they are.

✓ **Not enough follow-up**—Don't disappear on your clients. Even if you have other pressing business or other sales at crucial stages, make sure you stay in touch with all your clients so they always feel like you're thinking about them and their needs. Remember that clients need frequent reassurance. They're making a huge financial and emotional commitment. Everything may be running smoothly and their purchase may be at a stage where there's nothing they need to do, but it will help to hear you reassure them that everything is fine.

SHOWING HOMES

Once you're actually at the property you're showing, avoid overselling it. Less is more when showing a house. You will have already talked about the property and the neighborhood on the way over; now is the time to let the property sell itself. Be confident and reassuring but also understated. Your confidence will allay potential buyers' nervousness.

If the owners are present, you'll want to greet them politely and make sure that there aren't any last-minute problems you need to know about. But unless there are particular safety considerations, it's usually best to let the clients wander through the house at their own pace, spending as much or as little time as they want in each room. You want to stay nearby so you can answer questions, but the best way to sell a house during showing is to get out of the way and let the buyers sell it to themselves.

There will be plenty of time to talk about the house after you've left the property (and when the owners aren't nervously watching your every move and reaction).

Some tips for looking at houses:

✓ Bring flashlights. Keep several small but durable flashlights handy (the small Maglites™, with their metal cases, are a good choice). If there's a light bulb burned out in the basement or attic, you don't want it to ruin the walk-through.

✓ Wear comfortable and durable clothing. Wear shoes that will stand up to walking up narrow stairways and through muddy yards. Your clothing should be nice but not fragile—you will pick up a surprising amount of dust and dirt even in clean houses.

✓ Go first in potential trouble areas. If the basement has rickety-looking stairs, or there's a pull-down attic stairway, you'll want to try them first. Test the slippery-looking concrete around the pool before you let clients get too close to the water. Clients may be distracted, so it's important to warn about possible danger spots.

✓ Maximize the light. If there are curtains or blinds in the house, make sure to open them. (This also tells you whether they work properly.) Turn on the lights in each room. You want the house to have a bright, open feeling.

STAGING A HOUSE

The practice of "staging" high-end homes is growing, particularly in very fast-moving markets such as the Bay Area in California. Essentially, the property owner vacates the house and a specialized crew of interior decorators come in to paint, redecorate, or rework the house as necessary. The owner's furniture may be used, or it may be stored and rented furniture brought in. The idea is that by spending several thousand dollars on staging (typically the seller pays for the staging), you can make the house as appealing as possible to a high-end buyer and generate multiple offers at, or above, the asking price. Usually, this is worth the investment only on high-end properties that are expected to sell quickly.

REPEAT VISITS

When clients want to return to a particular house, it's even more important to not push them too hard. If they're returning to a property, you already know that they like it. They may want to compare it with something else they've seen, or see it at a different time of day to confirm that they like it as much as they remember. It can be difficult to stay restrained on repeat visits, especially as a new agent. You feel very close to a sale and want to hurry it along before something can go wrong; avoid the temptation to push your clients.

Second visits can be very long or very short. Sometimes buyers just want to confirm one particular thing about the property. At other times they want to crawl into every nook and cranny and pace around every wall like a cat in a new room. Let them take as long as they need without interference. Don't seem impatient or bored—the buyers may cut the visit shorter than they want out of politeness, and it could end up costing you a sale. If you can't share their excitement at the possibilities the house presents, then make yourself unobtrusive and stay in the background.

GETTING TO THE OFFER

Eventually the buyers will decide on a house that they like. The house either fits what they were looking for, or they have decided it's the closest combination of the things they wanted available in their price range. Now it's time to get them to make an offer on the house.

How quickly customers move varies from buyer to buyer, and from market to market. Every experienced real estate agent has stories of buyers who spent six months searching before they settled on a house. On the other hand, if you're working in a brisk real estate market where houses typically receive multiple offers in the first week they're listed, your clients may not have the luxury of making a leisurely choice.

Remember, your commission is secondary to the client's interest. Your job is to deliver the best situation for the client; let the commissions take care of themselves. There are too many transactions today where the agent is holding the transaction together with glue and duct tape just to preserve the commission rather than stopping to think about what is in the client's best interest. Agents who put the client's interest first prosper. Agents who follow a code of ethics and think in terms of fulfilling the fiduciary duties of putting their client's interests first and being faithful to that relationship, those are the people who prosper.

—RALPH TAMPER

GETTING BUYERS TO MAKE AN OFFER

Just because the buyers have chosen a house doesn't mean they've decided to make an offer. Many buyers get stalled at this key point, with emotional or other issues keeping them from actually committing to the house they want. At this point, it's appropriate to do some gentle nudging.

You don't want to make buyers feel like you are pushing them or giving them a hard sell. If they feel pressured, buyers may wonder why you're trying to rush them—and they will resist being railroaded. Too much pressure, badly timed pressure, or tactlessness on your part can kill the sale at this point, even though the buyers have decided on a house and are on the edge of committing money to their purchase.

The key is not to push buyers but to empower them—to help them finalize a decision they already want to make and to reassure them that this huge emotional and financial commitment is going to make a huge and positive difference in their lives.

What are some ways of accomplishing this?

✓ **Search for obstacles**—Are there any final obstacles preventing the buyers from making their decision? Find out what those obstacles are and see if you can suggest any solutions. For example, if they love the house but are reluctant to buy before a parent living halfway across the country sees it, you can arrange for a virtual tour of the house over the Internet. (See page 72.)

✓ **Get objections out in the open**—Is there something about the property the buyers aren't happy with? Find out what it is so you can address the problem. For instance, if the buyers are concerned about the town's reputation for having wells run dry, you might reassure them that they can have the seller agree to pay for well tests and any redrilling needed as a result of the tests as a condition of their offer. If the buyers have a list of questions, you can take those questions to the seller and get some answers.

✓ **Talk in a comfortable place**—Go over the property's strengths in a comfortable setting. If you're trying to get buyers to make an offer, talk to them in your office over coffee, not in the car or under a streetlight across from the property.

✓ **Tell the buyers if there's competition**—If you're in a hot market and they hesitate, there's a good chance they may lose the house. If houses in your area are receiving multiple offers in the first week they're listed, make certain your clients know that. If there are other bidders competing for the property, you can say that, too. But whatever you do, *do not lie about there being other bidders*. It may seem like a harmless way to make hesitant buyers commit, but the courts have also seen it as a fraudulent technique for driving up prices. Real estate agents have been taken to court and convicted for lying to buyers about their competition.

BUYERS AND SELLERS MEETING

You want to think long and hard before you let the buyers and the sellers meet. Unless you have a really compelling reason for having them to sit down together, it's probably a bad idea. The only time you should encourage the two parties to meet is if you think the sale will fall apart otherwise. Buyer-seller meetings are fraught with all sorts of problems from a real estate sales agent's point of view.

✓ If the sellers dislike the buyers, the sellers are unlikely to be flexible on price and will be reluctant to make any concessions that will facilitate a smooth sale, such as agreeing to leave the curtains or the ornamental birdbath that the buyer likes. In extreme cases the sellers may refuse to accept any offers from the buyers.

✓ If the buyers dislike the sellers, the whole deal is in trouble. If the buyers makes an offer at all, they are unlikely to be flexible or willing to bend in the direction of the sellers.

✓ If they get along, they are likely to keep talking with each other. While this may lead to a smooth agreement, it's also likely to lead to conversations that the real estate agents involved aren't aware of—which can easily lead to missing or fouled-up paperwork at closing time.

If the buyers and the sellers do meet, coach the buyers in what to say and what not to say.

✓ Buyers should be complimentary about the house but keep their enthusiasm to a minimum. If sellers know that the buyers must have this house, that it's their dream house, then any offer below the asking price is likely not to be agreed to. It's likely that the sellers will hold out for the asking price.

✓ If the buyers are planning on making significant changes to the house, they shouldn't talk about them to the sellers. They may be talking about destroying one of the sellers' favorite parts of the house. The exception to this is if the buyers need information about wiring or construction in order to make an informed decision about buying the house. That said, you, as the agent, can and should find out this kind of information from the sellers whenever possible.

✓ Sellers should not talk about the price of the house or hint at what price they would accept. That's the agent's job, and sellers could lose thousands of dollars by giving away that they'd accept less than the buyers were planning to offer.

✓ Look for common ground. For instance, if the buyers and the sellers both have children, the buyers can ask about raising kids in the house. Ideally, you want the sellers to feel that they're passing their home on to someone who will care about it as much as they did.

✓ Warn the buyers if there are particular topics to stay away from. If the house is being sold because of a bitter divorce, a bankruptcy, or a pending foreclosure, the sellers don't need the buyers reminding them about it.

If the buyers and the sellers don't get along (or worse yet, get into a fight), stay calm. Don't give up on the sale. Separate the two parties, talk to each of them, and remind them of what's important:

✓ It's more important to complete the sale than to win a fight. Even if both sides are sure they're right, is it worth losing the sale over?

✓ The buyers and the sellers don't have to be friends or even like each other, they just have to work together for a few weeks to complete the sale. If the sale is important, it's better for both sides to swallow their pride; after all, they never have to see each other again after the closing.

✓ If they can't stand to talk to each other or be in the same room with each other, that's fine. That's what the agents are there for, and you'll make sure their concerns are heard. (Remember that you'll have to get them both in the same room at closing, though.)

✓ Sometimes the two sides have just misunderstood each other. People say things they don't really mean when they're upset, distracted, or caught up in the emotional upheaval involved in buying or selling a house. If the buyers and the sellers are fighting over a simple misunderstanding, see if you can explain things to each side in a neutral way and defuse some of the emotions involved. If not, try to ignore it and not get caught up in other parties' petty melodramas.

✓ How would they look at things if they were in the other party's position? A successful sale should be fair to both sides, and arguments can erupt if one side thinks the other party is being unfair or ignoring legitimate concerns. Make sure both buyers and sellers know where the other party is coming from.

DIPLOMATIC SKILLS

The final stages of a sale call for a high level of tact and diplomacy on your part, regardless of whether you are representing the buyers, the sellers, or both parties. This is an emotional time for both sides, enormous amounts of money are being discussed, and both buyer and seller have given up most of their privacy to make the sale happen—sharing the details of their lives with bankers, real estate agents, and complete strangers. Tempers are apt to be running a bit high.

While one careless remark isn't likely to cost you a sale, a poorly chosen comment can easily offend one party or the other, cause delays and bad feelings, and make the unhappy party less flexible in the final negotiations. Watch what you say.

If you do make a mistake or say something tactless or undiplomatic, acknowledge it, apologize, and fix the mistake. The quickest and easiest way to fix a problem is to show that you understand what went wrong and are committed to making it right. Watch out for warning signs and address them quickly.

✓ **Someone is obviously upset at what you just said**—Did you accidentally misrepresent someone? Did something you said come out wrong, or was it taken the wrong way? Apologize and rephrase, being sure to be nonconfrontational: "I'm sorry. I think that came out wrong. What I meant was. . . ." Make sure that clients know that you didn't mean offense and also that they understand what you were trying to say. It's not enough to apologize successfully if you forget to make your point clearly and leave your clients placated but confused.

✓ **Someone is suddenly very quiet**—Ask if everything's okay. If you think you may have said something wrong, apologize, but find out what you did so you can avoid repeating the mistake. "I'm sorry. Did I do something wrong?" Make sure you *listen to the answer*. Clients will forgive you once if you make an effort to improve, but if you've been warned about something that *really* bothers your clients—such as habitually interrupting, or calling the client "Bob" when he hates any name but "Robert," or ignoring one member of a couple—and do it again, don't expect the clients to ever trust or respect you again.

Don't assume that it's a problem any time your clients get quiet, but always keep an eye on their body language and how comfortable they seem to be with what you're saying and how you're treating them.

Buyers expect their agent to be their advocate and to give them sound, concrete advice as to how they should negotiate and what they should ask for. Agents need to be skilled at educating the buyer about making reasonable requests of the property owners and sellers. Some people believe that the buyer agent's duty is to beat up the seller and the listing agent. Buyers lose houses that way. The reality is that the reasonable person wins. If the buyer wants to make an unreasonable request, you need to say, "Now, if you were the property owner, how would you respond to this?" and get them to think along those lines. It's not a war we're fighting. Buyers and sellers have a common goal.

—RALPH TAMPER

HOW TO GET CUSTOMERS TO MAKE THE RIGHT OFFER

When it comes to formulating offers, the role of buyer brokers and sellers' agents is dramatically different. As a buyer broker, you can help guide the buyers into picking the right offer and may discuss the strategy of what price to choose. If you represent the sellers, your job is to get the highest possible price for the sellers, and you're limited in what advice you can give the buyers without a conflict of interest.

Typically, a house sells for between 80 and 100% of its asking price. If a house is in an exceptionally hot market and there are multiple offers, it may sell for more than the asking price. Houses rarely receive offers for less than 80% of the final asking price, even in depressed markets, because most buyers think that anything less than that is insulting to the sellers.

If you are representing the sellers or acting as a dual agent for both buyers and sellers, you can give the buyers the following guidelines in formulating their offer:

✓ You can tell the buyers what the asking price is on the house and if there have been any reductions from the original price.

✓ If the seller has asked you to let buyers know he or she is flexible on the price you may do so, but otherwise you can't.

✓ If the buyers ask how long the house has been on the market you can tell them, but don't volunteer the information otherwise.

✓ If there are other offers or other potential buyers who are likely to make offers, you can say so, but only if you have the sellers' permission. However, you can't tell the buyers how much has been offered. You also can't misrepresent offers or claim there are other offers if there aren't. It's illegal.

✓   If you are a dual agent, you can't tell the sellers how much money the buyers have to spend, or whether you think the buyers are willing to raise an offer.

✓   Unless the sellers have specifically given you permission, you can't say if there are special circumstances forcing the sale, such as a divorce, bankruptcy, or impending foreclosure. Sometimes desperate sellers will ask you to disclose this information to hurry up a lagging sale, but otherwise it's off limits.

Be sure to specifically review your area's rules and regulations regarding what information seller's agents and dual agents are allowed to reveal to buyers.

If you are a buyer broker, you have more freedom to help your clients strategize. You may want to discuss the following issues:

✓   **Is the house overpriced?**—If the house is seriously overpriced and hasn't gotten any offers after a month on the market, your clients may be able to make a low offer and get a response, at least to a more reasonable counteroffer. If the sellers are unwilling to move, the clients have the choice of overpaying or moving on.

✓   **Is the house underpriced?**—If the house is selling below market value, the sellers are trying to move the house quickly (or they have an incompetent agent). An underpriced house is likely to sell at or above the asking price.

✓   **How long has the house been on the market?**—Has it been through several listing agents? If the house has been on the market for a long time, it may have been overpriced, or the owners may not have been eager to sell. Some owners get increasingly anxious as their house goes longer and longer without selling. Even owners who initially refused to budge off their price may become reasonable when the offers stop coming in.

✓ **How much has it come down in price?**—If the property was initially overpriced, have the sellers given indications that they're willing to accept a more reasonable figure? Have there been several price drops recently, signaling an increasing desire to move the property?

✓ **How desperate are the sellers to move the property?**—If the sellers are divorcing or have fallen into default on their mortgage, they are likely to accept a lower offer if your clients are in position to close the sale quickly.

✓ **Are other timing factors involved?**—Sellers may be willing to take less money if there are expenses about to come in, such as winter heating bills or property tax payments (generally due in January and July).

✓ **How much competition is there?**—Is this house likely to receive multiple offers, or are other serious buyers unlikely? Is the market for this type of property hot, or is the property likely to remain unsold if these particular buyers fall through?

FORMULATING THE OFFER

When formulating an offer, buyers are trying to find a balance between how much they can afford to spend and what's the lowest price they think the sellers will accept. Using tact and carefully explaining their offer to the sellers increases the likelihood of its being accepted (or at least of a reasonable counteroffer).

Here are a few guidelines to use when helping buyers put together their offers and when presenting those offers to the listing agent (or to the sellers, if you are the listing agent or a dual agent):

✓ Buyers should always have a reason for their offer. The buyers may have chosen the price because it's $15,000 below the asking price of $175,000 and the sellers aren't likely to get a better offer before winter sets in, but they should give a tactful explanation that seems to be giving something back to the sellers. For instance, "The house will need a new roof and updated wiring in the next couple of years, which will cost about $30,000, but we're willing to meet you halfway and bear half of that cost, so we're offering $160,000 and we'll bear the cost of the roof and wiring." The buyers are going to have to pay that cost anyway, but this way the sellers can feel there's a reason for the lower amount and it wasn't just chosen arbitrarily to try and squeeze a lower price out of them.

✓ If the offer is significantly below the asking price, the buyers shouldn't add a lot of contingencies into it. If they're getting a great deal on the house, they don't need to go after the furniture and appliances, too, or the owner will feel taken advantage of.

✓ It's a good idea to have some contingencies in the offer that the buyers are willing to give in on, especially if they don't have a lot of price flexibility. Make sure there's something that will make the sellers feel like they're winning something back in the negotiation (especially if they are very competitive). Buyers can easily give in to the sellers regarding time of closing or appliances, for instance, in order to close the deal.

✓ If the sellers are desperate or the market is slow, buyers can ask for many contingencies without seeming unreasonable. If the market is hot or the house has multiple offers, sellers may not want to be bothered with a lot of contingencies and may sell the house to bidders who present the least complicated offer, even if it's slightly below the highest offer.

✓ Make sure the buyers realize that their first offer may be accepted. They shouldn't put in contingencies just as negotiating points if they're not willing to live with them. If the buyers hate the curtains and the house has 40 windows, don't make keeping the curtains a contingency in the assumption that the sellers will want to take the $2,500 worth of curtains with them and they can be given up in the negotiating process. The sellers may be sick of the curtains, too, and the buyers will be stuck with the time and cost of taking down and disposing of a carload of ugly curtains.

"Insult" Offers

If you are representing the sellers, you are generally obligated to present all offers to your clients, even if they're unrealistically low. It's your clients' choice whether to accept or reject the offer, not yours. Every once in a while, clients will feel it's in their best interest to accept an offer below fair market value; the choice is the clients' and not yours.

Lowball offers fall into several categories:

✓ **Wake-up calls**—The offer may signal that the buyers see the house as overpriced. If the price they are offering is in the vicinity of market value, and the sellers aren't determined to get their price at all costs, a counteroffer with some movement may be a good idea.

✓ **Fishing expeditions**—Buyers may be looking to exploit the sellers to make a killing on the market, or buyers may sense that the sellers are very eager to sell. Chances are the buyers are hoping for a counteroffer with a significant drop in price, with a final price halfway between the offer and the asking price. If the sellers are not desperate to move the house quickly, you may want to explain to the buyers that the house is not going to sell for below market price and encourage a revised offer. Your clients can then make a counteroffer based on the second, higher offer.

✓ **Uninformed buyers**—Some buyers (or their agents) may seriously misread the market. If the house is fairly priced and likely to draw other offers near the asking price, you may want to suggest that buyers make an offer closer to market price, or your clients may reject the offer entirely.

✓ **Underfinanced buyers**—Sometimes buyers simply are not in a financial position to offer the asking price. The offer may be the best the buyers can afford, or close to it. If the house is unlikely to sell otherwise, or if the sellers have to move the property quickly, the sellers may want to consider a counteroffer slightly above the buyers' offer, to see if the buyers can afford to go any higher.

The next chapter contains strategies for bridging the gap between buyer and seller as well as getting from acceptance to closing successfully.

SUMMING UP

Showing houses is like matchmaking—your job is to pair up buyers and sellers who are a good match for each other. Remember that both buyers and sellers want the same thing: a successful and amicable transfer of the property.

Know your selling points and your neighborhoods. You should be comfortable talking about what each house has to offer your clients and what's special about the neighborhood it's situated in.

Remember your buyers' emotional needs. Buyers want to feel you care about them and their interests.

You should know what to expect when showing houses, and come prepared.

Don't pressure buyers to choose a particular house. After they've chosen a house, you can encourage them to make an offer quickly.

How offers are made and received varies dramatically depending on the market, as well as on the financial and emotional situations of both buyers and sellers. No matter what, it's important to stay tactful and reassuring to your clients.

CHAPTER 6

THE FINAL STAGES
OF THE SALE

- ◆ NOW THAT THE OFFER'S BEEN MADE, IT'S TIME TO GET FROM OFFER TO ACCEPTANCE. HOW DO YOU CLOSE THE GAP BETWEEN THE OFFER AND THE ASKING PRICE?

- ◆ WHAT ARE THE LAST-MINUTE DETAILS TO BE TAKEN CARE OF?

- ◆ HOW DO YOU GET BUYERS AND SELLERS AND LAWYERS AND BANKERS TO THE TABLE?

- ◆ WHAT ELSE DO YOU NEED TO KNOW TO ARRANGE THE TIMING SO IT ALL COMES TOGETHER AT ONCE—AND SO YOU CAN FIX THINGS IF THEY GO WRONG AT THE LAST MINUTE?

The time between the first offer and actually closing the deal on a house is a particularly precarious period. Now that the courtship is over and money is actually being discussed, both buyers and sellers are apt to be suspicious of each other and afraid of being taken advantage of. Under the tremendous emotional pressure of buying or selling a house, both parties are apt to be volatile or forgetful of key details in the last days before closing.

Your job at this time is to play peacemaker and keep track of all the details. No matter what happens, don't let yourself get caught up in the emotional upheavals and petty arguments that erupt as the sale draws near its close. Don't take sides. Don't criticize anybody involved in the process—including other agents, lenders, appraisers, lawyers, or home inspectors, not to mention buyers, sellers, and their relatives—no matter how frustrating their behavior may be to deal with. There is a very high possibility of your words being twisted around or misconstrued and coming back to haunt you at the closing table.

PRESENTING THE OFFER
TO THE SELLERS

The way you present an offer to the sellers is going to vary a little depending on if you are a sellers' agent or a dual agent. (If you are a buyer broker, you're more likely to be presenting the offer to the sellers' agent, who will present it to the sellers.) By now, the sellers are expecting an offer. All of their expectations and fears will be heightened. It's important that you help keep them grounded emotionally, preparing them for the offer before you present it, walking through what the offer means, and talking with them about what the best response should be.

A badly presented offer can create animosity and inflexibility; if there are bad feelings on one or both sides, there will be little of the give and take that a successful property sale often requires. Don't lose sight of the fact that the goal is not to *win* the negotiation—it's to have the property change hands with both sides satisfied that their emotional, financial, and physical needs were met.

On the other hand, a well-presented offer can create openings for both sides. Even if the offer is declined, both parties feel they are negotiating in good faith and will be willing to keep talking. Small differences are more likely to be resolved, and both parties can more easily keep the objective—a successful sale—in mind.

Presenting the Offer to the Sellers' Agent

If you're a buyer broker, you can help your chances of having an offer accepted by the sellers if you give their agent some tools to work with. Don't just tell the offer to the listing agent. Explain it and give him or her as many tools and arguments to take back to the sellers as possible. If you can convince the agent that the offer is reasonable, there's a good chance that the agent can convince the sellers likewise. (Of course, the same thing works in reverse for counteroffers: The listing agent needs to explain the offer thoroughly to the buyer broker.)

Always give a reason for any adjustment in price, so the other party doesn't feel that you're just arbitrarily trying to pay less than what they think is a fair price. Again, never say that a property is overpriced; instead, explain why your clients can't pay that price—even though it's reasonable. Some examples of how you might present an offer:

✓ If there is a major contingency, give a good reason for it. For instance, an FHA (Federal Housing Administration) mortgage might require that the house have a drilled well instead of a dug well, so the seller will have to pay for a new well prior to closing. Or the buyers might ask that the sellers replace the furnace and leave the appliances in the house, because if they meet the asking price of the house they won't have enough money left over to buy new appliances.

✓ If there is a major price deduction, give a plausible explanation for it. If the wiring is unsafe and will need to be replaced right away, explain that the offer had to be a little lower because the buyers need to be able to pay for rewiring before they can move in. You want the owners to think that the offer is lower than they hoped because the buyers are being forced to spend some of their money on repairs that they are not asking the seller to make, instead of thinking that they are just trying to haggle for a better price. In other words, you want the sellers to look at the money they are saving in potential repairs, rather than just focusing on the price the buyers are offering.

✓ Remove obstacles and try to put the sellers (and their agent) at ease before explaining a lower-than-expected price. For example, if you know that the sellers are worried about a bad door, let them know that it's not an obstacle, and then talk about the things that are positive, that the sellers want to hear: You're asking for a closing in December, that's no problem. We're not concerned about the driveway. We realize the property needs a new roof, and we've adjusted the price for that. Show how the offer is an attempt to bridge a gap between the price the sellers want and what the buyers need in a house.

✓   Remind the sellers of any positives in the offer that they might lose sight of by focusing on the price. For instance, if the buyers are able to pay cash, are preapproved, are willing to be particularly flexible about when they close or move in, or aren't asking for a lot of contingencies, make sure the sellers understand that not all buyers are so well prepared. They might hold out for another buyer who offers a little more money only to have the sale drag out and cost thousands of dollars more because that buyer is poorly prepared or asks for major contingencies.

✓   If the house has been on the market for a long time or has been through multiple real estate agents, the sellers may need to be gently reminded that there may not be any buyers who are willing to make a better offer for the house—and the cost of waiting may not be worth the wait. If the house has high heat or maintenance costs or is in a high-tax area, keeping the house on the market may be an expensive proposition if the offer received is a reasonable one.

PREPARING SELLERS FOR THE OFFER

If you are the listing agent, you should start preparing the sellers for an offer on the property as soon as you know that buyers are very interested and are likely to make a bid. You will need to prepare the sellers emotionally as well as intellectually. Until the offer is in hand, many sellers don't really understand that the buyers don't necessarily see the house the same way as do the sellers—who have lived there for years and may have grown up in the house. For some sellers, the emotional impact of selling their home hits only when an offer is received.

You will want to reassure the sellers, explain all the possibilities, and talk about how you might respond to each. The idea is not to depersonalize the process but to give the sellers a little bit of emotional distance to help them to understand the buyers' point of view, which may be very different from their own—and its value. Some things you will want to talk about include:

✓ Any kind of offer is possible. All sellers have a fantasy of what they hope the offer will be and a nightmare of what they fear it will be, but only buyers can decide what to offer.

✓ The offer may be great or it may be disappointing. It may be something the sellers can accept, or it may just be a starting point for negotiations.

✓ Don't take the offer personally. What a house sells for has a lot less to do with how the sellers have lived in it than it does on market forces and how much other houses in the neighborhood have sold for. A high or low offer doesn't reflect on the sellers personally, and they want to be careful not to respond to it in a different way from how it was intended. Nobody makes an offer on a house to insult the sellers; people make offers based on how much they think the house might sell for, and sometimes they misjudge.

✓ Explain the possible offers to the sellers, and give them an idea of what kind of offer is likely.

✓ Talk about possible contingencies that might be included in the offer. Explain what contingencies are likely, and talk about how they might respond. Are the washer and dryer important to them, or can they be thrown in to close a deal? If the buyers come in with a good price but want the sellers to replace the furnace, how will they respond? How strong a negotiation position are the sellers in? Talk through a number of scenarios, until the sellers are comfortable with the idea of contingencies and their role in the negotiating process.

✓   Get the sellers thinking in terms of concrete responses to possibilities, rather than their first emotional response to giving up their house.

✓   Try to avoid building up clients' expectations too much. Make sure they know both the best- and worst-case scenarios.

✓   While you are talking, be very reassuring and calm. Some of that serenity will gradually make its way to your clients. Discuss possible ideas with them until you're comfortable that they won't fall apart emotionally when you present the first offer to them.

EXPLAINING THE OFFER TO THE SELLERS

If you're the listing agent, once you have all the details of the offer from the buyers or their agent, you have to present that information to the sellers. Give some thought to what the best way to present that information is. How does it fit into the scenarios you discussed with the sellers previously? Is this a strong offer, a weak offer, or something in between? Remember that even a terrific offer presented poorly may cause the sellers to become upset, while they may react positively to a marginal offer that is clearly explained and presented.

Here are some strategies to think about for presenting the buyers' offer to the sellers.

✓   Explain any background information first, before you give the sellers the number. If you give them a low number and then try to explain, they may not hear you, because they're still in shock because the price wasn't what they'd hoped for or expected.

✓   At the same time, don't spend *too* long on the background explanations. Explain the buyers' concerns and financial situation, but don't take so long getting to the price that you seem to be stalling; don't leave your clients in suspense.

✓   Let the sellers vent their initial anger or frustration before you can discuss how to respond to the offer. They might have built up expectations, regardless of what you said to them earlier. They may be upset if the offer is low or has many contingencies.

✓   Act as a sounding board, if necessary. Make sure that the sellers remember that the final price has to be fair for both sides. Even if the sellers are unhappy with the buyers now, an angry or inflexible response is not going to get their house sold. Make sure that you explain the buyers' point of view, so you can begin talking about a possible solution that works for both sides.

✓   Think about possible responses. If the sellers are in a strong negotiating position, you may want to talk with them about strategies for responding. This will help get the sellers thinking in terms of making a deal happen, instead of focusing on their disappointment with the initial offer.

✓   If at all possible, present the offer to the sellers in person. You will have a lot more control over the situation, and you can act as a calm and reassuring presence. You will be much less able to defuse crises over the phone. If the sellers are not local, or if you have to present the offer by phone for other reasons, be careful that you have prepared the sellers properly beforehand. Avoid presenting offers by e-mail unless absolutely necessary. The possibility of misinterpretation by sellers is very high.

RESPONDING TO THE OFFER

Sellers can choose to respond to an offer in several different ways. They may accept the offer, accept it with conditions, make a counteroffer, or reject the offer outright. If you are a dual agent, representing both buyers and sellers, your role in guiding the sellers and giving them advice on how to respond will be limited. If you are acting exclusively as the sellers' agent, you can be much more specific in discussing options with them, without fearing a conflict of interest.

As the sellers' agent, your job at this point is to secure the best bottom line for your clients, while remembering that the most successful sales are the ones where the deal works for both sides. Remember that the best deal doesn't always mean the best price; sometimes it's better to take a slightly lower offer that doesn't burden the sellers with difficult or expensive contingencies. You have to look beyond the effect on your commission and consider what factors are most likely to make the sale work for both sides. A great price that leads to bad feelings and recriminations at closing isn't worth the extra few dollars in commissions—especially since it will cost you any potential referrals that this sale might have led to.

What response should you make to an offer?

✓ **Acceptance**—If the offer is fair, within the price range that your clients are hoping for, and doesn't have any unreasonable or burdensome conditions, the sellers may want to accept it.

✓ **Conditional acceptance**—If the offer is close to what the sellers are looking for financially, but some of the other terms or conditions need adjustment, the sellers may want to accept conditionally. For instance, if the buyers offer a good price but want to close within two weeks, the sellers might accept, on the condition that the buyers agree to take care of hauling away junk that the sellers will not be able to get to in two weeks.

✓ **Counteroffer**—If the offer is below the sellers' acceptable price range, but not outrageously so, and doesn't have unreasonable or burdensome conditions, the sellers may want to counteroffer. If you present a counteroffer to the buyers or their agent, always attach a condition or explanation why the sellers are willing to accept a lower offer. Emphasize that the sellers are willing to reduce the price because of some aspect of the buyers' offer, not because the asking price was too high.

For example, if the asking price of the house is $165,000 and the buyers offer $155,000, with no stipulations, the sellers may counter with $161,000, with the explanation that since the sellers don't have to spend $4,000 to have the house repainted for the buyers, they can lower their asking price by that amount.

✓ **Rejection**—If the offer is less than 80 percent of the asking price or is filled with unreasonable conditions, the sellers may want to reject the offer politely. If it is handled right, a rejection does not mean that the sale is dead. Just because an offer is too far away to be worth a counteroffer doesn't mean there won't be a revised—and more reasonable—offer. You need to politely (and nonconfrontationally) explain to the buyers or their agent that their price just wasn't in the range you need, or that they asked for something that the sellers weren't able to give. Be sure to make it clear that the sellers would love to sell the house to the buyers if the differences between the two parties' ideas can be worked out, and that you would welcome a revised offer.

✓ **Reject with an invitation to raise the offer**—Here the sellers decline the offer with an invitation to the buyers to submit another offer that is more in line with the current market conditions. This shows that the sellers may be amenable to the buyers' subsequent fair offer.

NEGOTIATING POINTS

When you're working with the sellers to formulate a response to the potential buyers' offer, think about what strengths you have in the negotiations. While in theory there may be many similar properties that the buyers can make offers on, in practice there are usually very few properties that will meet most of their needs. Your response to the buyers' offer should emphasize how well the property matches with their lives, regardless of whether their offer is conditionally accepted, countered, or declined. (If their offer is accepted outright, none of this is necessary.)

Do the buyers really need to have *this* property for some reason? Does it offer a particular feature that's important to them that they're unlikely to find elsewhere? Is it unlikely that another sale will work with their time frame? All of these are factors that might put you in a strong position in responding to an offer. In other words, the more perfect the house is for the buyers, the fewer concessions you will have to make on price. Some things to keep in mind:

✓   **Schools**—Do the buyers have children in school, or are they educators or school administrators? If so, they will want to complete the sale before the school year starts, so they may be under time pressure. If the house is in a strong school district and few other properties are available in that district, that's also a negotiating point, as is a school that is within walking distance for their children.

✓   **Appliances**—First-time home buyers are unlikely to have appliances and may not have the money or time to go hunting for new ones while they are trying to move into a new home. Leaving the appliances in place may be a major negotiating point, whether they are new or not. Even if the washer is on its last legs, you may be able to argue that it will be something else the buyers won't have to spend money on right now, and in a year when it dies they will be in a better financial position.

✓   **Employment**—If the buyers are moving to the area for employment, they will be under time pressure. Temporary housing is expensive, and buyers won't want to be unsettled any longer than necessary. Some jobs, such as many municipal, administrative, teaching, police, or firefighting positions, require employees to have local residency within a certain time as a condition of employment.

✓   **Religion**—If the buyers are religious, proximity to a church, synagogue, mosque, or other place of worship may be a factor. For example, most Orthodox Jews avoid driving on the Sabbath, so a synagogue within walking distance is a major consideration. Even if the buyers are not particularly observant themselves, a place of worship nearby where their children can walk to Sunday school can be an important negotiating point.

✓ **Other time factors**—Are there other reasons why the buyers need to move quickly? Have they already sold another house? Are they living with in-laws, with all the embedded tensions that involves? Are they kenneling pets? If the buyers are from out of town, do they need to complete the sale before flying back to their current home, or else have the expense of another house-hunting trip?

✓ **Uniqueness**—Is the property a one-of-a-kind house for which there are no comparable local properties? If the house is the only one for sale in the area that fulfills an important condition the buyers are looking for, such as handicap access in place, a separate in-law house, a barn with a water line to it, or required special zoning, then the sellers have added leverage.

✓ **Time limits**—Buyers sometimes include time limits in their offers, in an attempt to put pressure on the sellers to accept quickly. Usually these time limits can be ignored. If the buyers really want the house, they're not going to back out of the sale over an arbitrary time limit. There are many reasons why buyers or sellers may feel pressure to finish a sale quickly, but time limits are not among those reasons.

If you're in a strong position and don't feel you need to budge on price, you can make a counteroffer with other concessions, to show that while you think the price is fair, you do want to work with the buyers and are responsive to their needs. For instance, you might say that "the sellers really don't feel they can sell the property for less than $199,000, given how much other properties around here are selling for and how much they had to spend on the new furnace last year. But we can close on a month from Thursday the way you want, and your electricians can start work before closing the way you want, as long as they sign a damage waiver and you agree to pay them for the job no matter what, so the sellers aren't left with a half-wired house if you back out of the sale before closing."

MULTIPLE OFFERS

If the house is in a fast-moving market, you may receive multiple offers. From the sellers' point of view, multiple offers are an ideal situation. The presence of competition almost guarantees that the house will draw a price near—or even above—the asking price. Work closely with the sellers to evaluate each offer, looking carefully at the conditions in each. Remember that the highest price isn't always the best offer, when the cost and hassle of the conditions are figured in.

If you are representing the buyers instead of the sellers, be very reluctant to get into multiple-offer situations. While it's unavoidable in some markets, the presence of more than one potential buyer can lead to conflicts and to bidding wars that result in buyers paying too much for houses.

If your clients are among several people bidding on this house, you want to focus on being perceived as the *best* bidder, whether your offer is the highest or not. (Of course, your offer will have to at least be in the ballpark to be considered, but don't let your clients be drawn into over-bidding if there are other houses available that would meet their needs just as well.) Here are some factors that will make your clients' bid an attractive one:

✓ **Strong financial position**—If there is more than one bidder, your clients will need to be preapproved at a minimum, not just prequali-fied. If there is more than one bidder, buyers who can close quickly and without obstacles will win out over clients who have to haggle with a lender for a month before the details of a mortgage can be finalized.

✓ **Good fit for the house**—Do the sellers feel that your buyers would be perfect for the house? Do they think the buyers would be able to appreciate the property the way they did? All things being equal, would they rather have your clients living in the house than any of the other bidders?

✓ **Respectful of the sellers**—Have your clients been pleasant and polite to the sellers? Did their bid reflect the sellers' needs and not try to take advantage of the sellers? Have you been tactful and helpful to the sellers in your role as the buyers' agent? Are there other signs that if they accept your clients' offer it will lead to a smooth, trouble-free closing?

✓ **No burdensome conditions**—Are your clients asking the sellers for contingencies that will be expensive, time-consuming, or unpleasant to do? Are there too many contingencies to reasonably get done before closing? Look at any conditions from the sellers' point of view before your clients finalize their offer.

COUNTEROFFERS

Buyers should be prepared for counteroffers the same way sellers need to be prepared for offers. (See page 112.) When the buyers respond to a counteroffer, be sure to give a reason or an added condition to justify any increase in price offered. Otherwise, the sellers may feel that you could have offered more in your original offer and may be upset. For instance, if the buyers offer $184,000 on a house that lists at $199,500, and the sellers responded with a $195,000 counteroffer, you might respond with an offer of $189,000, on the condition that the sellers leave the kitchen appliances and the red drapes in the living room. The sellers might accept that offer, accept it with conditions, or make a further counteroffer.

Make certain to be open and pleasant in your offers and counteroffers. Give the impression that everything will be settled, and remind your clients that all of the back and forth is just part of the normal, friendly negotiating process. Try to keep your clients from giving in to frustration if the process drags out. Encourage them to be as flexible as possible and to think of things from the sellers' point of view as well as their own. Unless the sale is fair for both buyer and seller, it probably won't happen.

AFTER THE COUNTEROFFER

As long as the counteroffers are made in good faith, and you make certain that all sides are focused on working together to make the sale happen, several rounds of offers are not a problem. Try to keep your clients friendly and focused; encourage them not to put emotional "time limits" on their offers or get upset if things don't immediately work out. The objective is to have a deal that satisfies both parties.

There are some things to keep in mind after the first round of offers has been exchanged.

✓   If you are a buyer broker, be careful not to let the buyers get ahead of themselves. Often buyers who are tough negotiators at first will begin to think they are almost in the house after the first offer and will accept almost any counteroffer. If there are important conditions that haven't been met in the counteroffer, the buyers shouldn't be afraid to ask for them, as long as they accompany the request with further movement on their own part.

✓   If you represent the sellers, take advantage of the buyers' tendency to get excited. After the first counteroffer, additional offers should be in smaller increments. If the sellers moved $5,000 on the first offer, the second offer should move perhaps half that and maybe as little as $1,000 to $2,000. Offers can be accompanied by other minor concessions that are attractive to buyers who are already eager to be in the house. If it's possible to whet their appetites further in the counteroffers, do so; if you know the buyers admired the yard and love gardening, offer to leave the lawn mower and lawn tools, which will remind them of the beautiful yard that they could soon be enjoying.

✓   Remember that the deal takes as long as the deal takes. If it's a hot market or there are other legitimate reasons to push a deal quickly, you may want to expedite things gently, but otherwise it's better to make sure both parties are satisfied that they're getting what they want and being treated fairly, even if it requires an extra round or two of calls on your part or an extra hour or two of explaining offers. The more comfortable both parties are that the negotiations have been fair and equitable, the better the chances for a smooth closing.

PREVENTING CLASHES

The agent has to encourage respect and consideration for the other party. There's no magic formula, other than making certain that people respect each other's position, and getting people to be reasonable, and never asking the other side to do something you wouldn't do if you were on the other side. That sounds like a terrible oversimplification, but it really is the secret to conflict resolution. If conflict does arise, you need to deal with it immediately, because it's like an infection, it grows. You need to get people to be as objective as possible. You need to defuse the emotions, help them identify alternatives, and when there is a problem, to let them vent on you. Then you can help them find a resolution that will be fair and equitable to all parties and they can ask for what they want in a reasonable and respectful way.

—RALPH TAMPER

BRIDGING THE GAP

Eventually buyers and sellers agree on a price and any conditions for the sale, and the buyers put down a deposit on the house. This may take several rounds of counteroffers, or it may happen almost immediately. The next part of the sale process—the interim between the agreement and closing the sale—is a tricky time. The details may have been settled, but many things still need to be taken care of before the sale actually can be completed—any one of which can jeopardize the closing if not done in a correct and timely way. The property will need to be appraised and inspected. The contingencies will need to be handled. The title search and any other legal issues will have to be resolved. The lender will have to be kept informed. Buyers and sellers will need to be kept happy and working toward their common goal of completing the sale.

Once the contract is written (in some regions by the agent and in others by a lawyer) and dates are put on it, you need to be certain your clients hit those dates. While it's possible to get an extension in some cases, every change or extension complicates the deal slightly and increases the chances of something going wrong or of bad feelings developing on one side or the other.

MAKING SURE THE SALE GOES THROUGH

If you are a buyer broker or sellers' agent, you will want to work closely with the agent for the other party to make sure everything gets done. (If you're a dual agent, you'll have your work cut out for you.) However, unless you know and have worked with this agent before, you'll still want to personally make sure that every stage is taken care of—don't just assume everything is all right because the agent assures you things are flowing smoothly.

Here are some tips to help get you through the period between agreement and closing.

✓ Make sure that you're *very* organized during this stage, because there's a good chance that the buyers and the sellers won't be. In the middle of the chaos and emotional strain involved in moving the property, your clients are apt to forget things or leave things undone. Keep notes on *everything*. Follow up frequently.

✓ Strongly consider giving your clients a checklist of the things they need to do, along with the dates they have to be done by. Keep your own master copy of the checklist, and check things off as you confirm that they've been done. Your version of the checklist should also include the lender, inspector, appraiser, lawyer (if there's a lawyer involved in the sale), and anyone else who needs to get something done before closing. Again, follow up frequently. Don't just assume that things are being done on time.

✓ Keep track of the contingencies and make sure everything's getting done. For example, the sellers may procrastinate on their promise to paint the house because packing for their move is going slowly. If you have to arrange to have junk hauled away yourself, do it. Make sure you have the numbers of reliable backup contractors who can be called in if things need to be pulled together at the last minute. You'll want to have pricing and information at your fingertips— who can haul trash to the dump for $10 an hour, who can rewire a room for $50 a receptacle, who can fix the nagging drips on the faucets for $30 each. Don't be afraid to get your hands dirty if that's what it takes to get all the details taken care of.

✓ Make sure all the legal details are taken care of. Has the title search been done and any potential complications cleared up? Are any necessary permits on file? If any significant work is being done to the house, local permits probably are required, and the building inspector may need to look at any work. If any of the property is considered wetlands, separate wetlands permissions also may be needed for any work.

✓ Keep on top of the lender to be certain all the details of the mortgage are in place. You don't want to find out there's a key document missing from the file causing the mortgage has fallen through on the day before closing.

✓ Be certain the appraiser and home inspector (see the next two sections) are scheduled to see the house, and the buyers knows when they will be seeing the property. Encourage the buyers to be at the property for the home inspection.

✓ Arrange for the buyers and sellers to get copies of all documents 48 hours ahead of closing for examination. That will give you time to make sure any errors get fixed. Check with both parties to be sure they have looked over the documents and don't have any questions; this is not something you want to wait until the closing to find out. Check over the papers yourself, as well. Are all the numbers right? Double-check the interest rate, closing costs, loan terms, and other figures that could easily be mistranscribed.

✓ Make sure the buyers know how much money to bring to closing.

THE APPRAISER

Another area where you'll want to use some strategy is the appraisal. Typically, the appraisal is done after the buyers and the sellers have agreed on a price but before the mortgage is finalized. Any appraiser who is on the lender's approved list may be used; in practice, there will be a short list of appraisers whom you trust to do the job right. (Ask another agent if you don't know which appraiser to use.) Appraisal is one area where the buyers and the sellers have little say; it doesn't really matter to the lender whether the buyers like the appraiser or not.

The appraiser will select a list of recently sold houses in the same neighborhood that are comparable to the property being sold. How well the property compares to those recently sold houses will determine its price. In practice, appraisers don't have a lot of time and often will rush the search. If there is a particular comparison you want to make sure is used—for instance, a house on the same block with the same number of rooms that sold for a very favorable price—make certain you point that house out to the appraiser. It makes the appraiser's life easier and makes your chances of a favorable appraisal much better. Be careful, though: If you suggest a house that isn't really comparable in order to try to inflate the appraisal, that appraiser will never trust you again and is likely to pass word along to the lender.

Before the house is appraised, you'll want to make sure both buyers and sellers understand the process thoroughly. An appraisal is not an absolute value judgment about the quality of a home. It's an estimate of what the current market value of that home is.

In certain situations, you'll want to have the appraisal done at a different stage of the home-buying process.

✓ If the buyers really want an overvalued house, and the sellers seem eager to sell, it may be worth the risk of having an appraisal done before the offer is made. If you let the sellers know that your clients want to make an offer but are unable to get a loan for more than the house's appraised value, the sellers may agree to consider an offer based on that value. When the offer is made, it puts the blame for the low price on the appraiser, not the buyers: "We think it's a beautiful house and is worth the asking price, but the bank will only approve a loan based on a value of $169,500, so that's all we can offer."

✓ Sometimes you have to postpone an appraisal until a lending problem is straightened out. If there are problems with the lender and you think it's likely the buyers will be shifting to a different lender, it's a good idea to put off the appraisal. If the appraisal is done but the appraiser isn't on the new bank's approved list, the buyers could end up having to pay for a second appraisal.

Make sure the buyers request a copy of the appraisal from their lender. The buyers are paying for it; it's their right to have a copy. It will also answer any lingering questions they have about how the process works.

If the appraisal comes in low, the sale is in serious trouble. As an agent, your options are pretty limited.

✓   You can ask for a new appraisal, but only if you have a particular
     reason to believe that the appraiser made a mistake that seriously
     deflated the house's value, such as miscounting the number of bed-
     rooms or leaving off outbuildings that are in good condition and
     clearly usable. The lender will not take kindly to your quibbling
     over small differences in valuation, and you're possibly asking the
     buyers to throw good money after bad, so unless you've got a
     smoking gun, you probably should accept the appraisal you've
     been given.

✓   You can revisit the offer and make a revised offer that's within the
     boundaries of the appraisal. At this stage—after the sellers have
     set their hearts on the agreed-on price—unless the sellers are real-
     ly desperate, a revised offer is unlikely to be accepted.

THE HOME INSPECTOR

The home inspector may be the biggest hurdle between the time a price is
agreed on and the sale's closing. The job of the home inspector is to go
through the property with the buyers (it is *very* important that the buyers
attend the home inspection) for several hours and make certain everything
is sound in the house. A good home inspector will explain the house to
potential buyers. For instance, instead of just making sure the furnace is
functional and safe, a good inspector will show the buyers how to maintain
the furnace and explain when to have it cleaned to maximize its life.

If you suspect there's a particular problem with the house—for example, if there's prior insect damage or if the electricity is suspicious—you
may want to recommend a home inspector who is especially strong in that
area. Otherwise, recommend a home inspector who matches the buyers'
personality well. You should become familiar with four or five inspectors
and their strengths. (Ask other agents for recommendations initially).
Most licensed home inspectors will do a pretty good job.

If the property is an older house, make sure the buyers realize that it
won't be perfect, as a new house might. Older houses will show signs of

wear and aging, even if they're in terrific condition. A 250-year-old house will almost invariably have powder-post beetle damage in the basement; the buyers need to know that as long as the infestation isn't active, it's not a reflection on the house.

If a home fails inspection, the chances of the sale going through are pretty slim. If the problem is comparatively minor and the sellers move aggressively in offering to fix it—for instance, a radon problem—the sale might be rescued. But often, if the buyers balk at buying the house after a so-so inspection, it's just an excuse; the buyers already had cold feet about the purchase and seized on the inspection as a reason. This is particularly common if the buyers feel railroaded into making an offer on a property they still had doubts about.

Once in a while you'll find buyers who don't want an inspection. For whatever reason—maybe because the buyers trust their own expertise, or they are suspicious of outside help, or they don't want to spend the money—some buyers want to go ahead with the sale without having the property professionally inspected. You should *strongly* discourage your clients from buying without an inspection. If lawyers or other trusted counselors are involved in the sale, see if you can enlist them to help convince the buyers. If all else fails and the buyers are determined not to have the property inspected, ask them to sign a letter stating that your advice to use a home inspector has been declined. Don't make a big deal of the letter; treat it just as another one of the many documents being signed. But if the buyers find problems a year after the sale, blame you, and threaten litigation, you'll be glad to have that letter in your files.

WHAT TO LOOK FOR IN A HOME INSPECTOR

A good home inspector will look at a house and find everything wrong with it that is humanly possible to find and at the same time have enough people skills so he doesn't scare people. If someone's buying a house that is a hundred years old, they shouldn't be surprised if they find that it's not perfect, because it's not going to be. It's just a question of how imperfect it is. You want to recommend home inspectors that are technically sound, with the ability to both communicate and put people at ease.

—RUSS HICKS

BEFORE THE CLOSING

Once you've reached the eve of the closing, you're in the home stretch. If you have been organized and done your homework to this point, you should be able to bring the sale together—and you'll be looking at a substantial payday shortly.

There are still a few steps before closing:

✓ Double-check every detail. This is your last chance to fix any mistake that you have missed. Be sure that all the paperwork is filled out properly and everything that belongs in the file is there. Have any details that have to be left until the end of the process—such as working out the oil adjustment if the house has oil heat—been taken care of? Is any required insurance in place?

✓ Make sure everything is done on the property or will be ready before the walk-through. If there's anything the sellers won't be able to finish in time, you'll need to bring in reinforcements—and if that means you have to go over to scrape and paint the peeling front door that the sellers meant to get around to, do it. If you need to rent a pickup and haul the trash to the dump, do it.

✓ Make sure the buyers have all the money they need to close, in an appropriate form, such as bank checks. Be certain they haven't miscounted, or written an amount in wrong—you don't want the closing on a half-million dollar property to be delayed because the buyers are several hundred dollars short.

✓ Check with the lender and the lawyer (if there is one) to make sure that everything is in order and that no one has written the wrong time on his or her schedule. Make sure the lender will be in the office during the closing in case you need to call to fix a last-minute hitch.

✓ Make certain that the buyers and the sellers know where they're supposed to be and at what time. Give people directions if they need them. If either party has a history of lateness, you may want to arrange to pick them up and take them to the closing, or give them a starting time half an hour before the actual scheduled closing. If they question the time change, simply tell them that you need to go over documents with them.

✓ If your clients have children or elderly parents, make sure they have arranged for care for longer than the anticipated closing time. If there's a problem and the closing takes six hours, you want your clients to be able to concentrate on getting the problem solved, not on who's watching the kids.

✓ Reassure both buyers and sellers that everything is going well and that this is a fair deal for both sides. Do what you can to soothe any tensions or calm any preclosing jitters.

LAWYERS

In some areas, no one would think of buying a house without a lawyer. In other areas, lawyers are uncommon at closings. Sometimes lawyers do valuable work and save everyone time and money; however, every once in a while, you will encounter a lawyer who feels that his or her role in the sale is to be obstructive and argumentative and to run up fees for his or her client.

A few things to keep in mind:

✓ If you're in an area where lawyers are uncommon during home sales and one party or the other wants to use a lawyer, don't raise any objection. It's their money, and clients who come from an area where lawyers are used in closings may feel uncomfortable without one. If your clients are not using a lawyer and the other party is, make sure to reassure your clients that just because someone uses a lawyer doesn't mean they're going to be taken advantage of. Don't let any suspicions build up that will affect the sale.

✓ If your clients are confused or uncomfortable with the buying or selling process, you should encourage them to use a lawyer, even in areas where it's uncommon. The cost of a lawyer—typically less than $1,000 for a closing—is well worth the peace of mind of knowing that everything has been taken care of by an expert.

✓ Never discourage a customer from seeking the services of a competent real estate attorney.

THE WALK-THROUGH

Often buyers and sellers will walk through the house together on the morning of the closing, to make sure both parties are satisfied that the house is as agreed on and all conditions have been met. You will want to be at the walk-through, to put out any fires and defuse any last-minute misunderstandings. There may be some confusion about what will happen during the closing, so you may want to explain and reassure everyone again.

✓ If you represent the buyers, arrange to meet them just before the walk-through. Make sure they've had coffee or juice and are not grumpy from low blood sugar. Be upbeat but don't lay it on too thick—this is a serious commitment for the buyers and they're likely to be in a serious mood.

✓ If the buyers or the sellers are not morning people, avoid chatter. Answer their questions, but follow their cue about how much to talk. Don't feel the need to fill pauses or silences in the conversation; many people prefer quiet first thing in the morning.

Don't worry too much if there's a problem—concentrate on fixing the problem, not laying blame or panicking at the potential consequences. At this point, things are pretty far along. A major problem might make for a long, frustrating closing. It might mean all parties (and their agents) have to make some last-minute concessions to get things done. But it's unlikely to kill the sale at this point if you address it promptly rather than trying to lay blame.

SMOOTH CLOSINGS

If you've done your job right, nothing should come up at the closing table. The closing is pretty much run by the attorneys and the bankers. Any real problems should have been worked out before you get there. We may have had a cantankerous time with the buyers and the sellers, and they may be emotionally upset with each other for one reason or another, but usually most closings go quite well. My advice to my salespeople is, when they go to closings, just be polite and try to keep the conversation flowing— because in many cases people are nervous—and let the lawyers and bankers do their job.

—RUSS HICKS

CLOSING THE SALE

Many people think of the closing as the climax of a home sale, but usually that's not true. If you've been organized and kept things running smoothly all along, the closing is likely to be routine and unexciting. Everyone will check the papers again, documents will be signed, payments will be handed over, and the property will legally change hands.

Even if it's likely that everything will go smoothly at closing, *you need to be there*. This is not the time to delegate or assume that nothing can go wrong. The sale isn't complete until after the closing; don't make the mistake of assuming your job is done. If you're not at the closing, your clients may feel abandoned. Even if things do go smoothly, clients who feel you weren't around at a crucial moment aren't going to send referrals your way.

Focus on the things you can do to keep the closing running smoothly.

✓ Make sure all the paperwork is there and no one has forgotten anything. If possible, stop by the location of the closing a few hours early to make sure all the details are in place.

✓ Bring extra pens and notepads for everyone; don't assume everyone will come to the closing with writing supplies. Buyers and sellers will be able to jot down any last-minute details if necessary. And having a scratch pad to doodle on may help clients ease nervous tension while talking or waiting for someone else to finish rereading a document during closing—tension that might otherwise spill over into a poorly chosen remark.

✓ Make sure there's coffee (or whatever each party likes to drink) and something light to nibble on. It will ease tensions, give people something to do other than fidget, and remind them that you have their interests in mind and take a personal interest in what they care about.

✓ Keep everything moving along. Be friendly, but if someone gets sidetracked or starts telling unrelated stories, gently bring him or her back on topic. The faster the closing goes, the less chance there is that discord will surface.

✓ If the buyers or the sellers have legitimate questions, make sure they're answered. Don't try to railroad people through the sale, or make them feel stupid for not having thought of the questions earlier. A person who feels he or she is being railroaded may get angry or suspicious enough to call the whole process to a halt.

✓ If the buyers and the sellers have clashed earlier, make sure that you take steps to minimize the friction. Make sure your clients are not left alone; if possible, you want to be with them to lend encouragement and to keep the focus away from their dislike of the other party. Buyers and sellers who don't get along should be seated at inconvenient angles to each other (such as on the same side of the table, with bankers and lawyers in between) so they can't glare at each other across the table until the tension simmers into an open fight.

If something goes wrong at closing, it's more likely to be due to a personality clash than due to a substantive problem. If you've handled all the details along the way, much of your task at closing is to keep everybody soothed and reassured, and to make sure both buyers and sellers are focused on completing the sale and not on their feelings about each other.

SUMMING UP

Try to keep your clients from being too emotional about offers and counteroffers. Make sure you always give the other party a reason for any change in price when you make an offer or counteroffer.

After the price is agreed on, you need to be especially well organized. A lot has to be done between the time the contract is signed and the closing—but if you keep things flowing and on time, the closing will be fairly painless.

If everybody is focused on the common goal of moving the property, most closings are unexciting and anticlimactic. If you've made sure all the details are handled, any problems at closing are likely to be from ruffled feathers or emotions running high.

CHAPTER 7

AFTER THE SALE

+ HOW DO YOU MAKE CERTAIN BOTH BUYERS AND
  SELLERS ARE SATISFIED?

+ HOW DO YOU TURN SATISFIED CLIENTS INTO
  REFERRALS AND OTHER NEW CLIENTS?

As mentioned throughout this book, your best source for new sales is satisfied buyer clients and customers. Your best referrals will be people who have a friend, relative, or neighbor who bought a house from you—and who was happy with the experience. This chapter contains some guidelines for making sure the people who buy houses from you are happy with the experience—and stay happy.

After the sale has closed, it is important to make sure that the buyers are satisfied. Find out if there's anything still unsettled or any other way that you can be helpful. Let the buyers know that you're still around if they need you—that you aren't going to disappear from their lives now that you've been paid for the sale.

However, this doesn't mean that you should nag the buyers five minutes after they've left the closing table. You can call them once they've moved in, or stop by to see how their improvements to the house are going. Or, pop in with a modest, yet thoughtful housewarming gift, such as a plant. The idea is to remind them that you're a positive part of their lives whom they associate with good things happening to them—and one whom they won't hesitate to recommend to others.

ASKING FOR REFERRALS

It's not enough to assume that satisfied buyers will send referrals your way. You actually have to ask people to refer you. Sometimes it never even occurs to buyers that real estate agents are always looking for referrals.

That said, never be blunt or tactless when asking for a referral. You can ask directly, but there are subtler and friendlier ways. Send a card to buyers a few weeks after they move into their new house. Thank them for their business and for their trust in you. Mention that when they hear about anyone else who is looking for real estate help, you'd be happy to talk to them. Be sure to enclose a few business cards, and encourage them to distribute them among friends and family who may be in need of the services of a real estate professional.

Sometimes a letter can work better. Brokers Pat and Ed Farthing send letters after the closing to thank buyers. In the body of the letter, they remind the customers just how important they are to their business. They come right out and say something to the effect of "customers like you recommend us to your friends and relatives, and that's the reason that we've had a successful real estate career, and we hope that you will refer us." A high percentage of these satisfied customers call the Farthings immediately afterward to refer other people to them. Remember, most people are happy to make personal recommendations because they appreciate how difficult it is to find good service these days. Think about the referrals you make all the time: for a baby-sitter, a tailor, a lawn mower, a hardwood floor refinisher, and so on.

GIFTS TO BUYERS

Many real estate agents give small gifts to buyers after they move in. Like freebies that you give to prospective customers (page 59), the idea is to give something useful that will help the buyers to remember you and associate you with the positive experience of moving into their new house.

Gifts should be small (the Internal Revenue Service allows up to $25 as a deductible expense per gift) and appropriate for a housewarming. You don't want to make the buyers feel like they're obligated to you. Make sure to include several extra cards with your present. Note that in some areas, gifts from real estate agents are frowned on.

Some gift ideas:

books on topics of local interest
candles
chocolates
coffee mugs and gourmet coffee basket
dinner gift certificate
fruit basket
houseplants
pottery
specialty vinegars or cooking oils
teapot and gourmet tea basket
wine

If you don't want to give a gift with monetary value, you can show clients you're grateful for their business in other ways. For instance, you can take the buyers out to dinner at a local restaurant in their new neighborhood. This gives them a chance to discover something about their new hometown as well as reinforcing what you helped them with.

FOLLOWING UP

Continue to keep in touch with past clients, even long after the sale. Referrals often will come years later, if you've remained fresh in people's minds. While you don't want to pester people, a good rule of thumb is that former clients should hear from you at least once a year.

Don't restrict yourself to former clients, either. If there are people you showed houses to and built a rapport with (e.g., another agent's clients who looked at one of your listings), keep them on your mailing list, even if they didn't actually buy a house through you. Sometimes the people who send you the most referrals are not the ones who bought a property from you but those who bought through another agent and *wish* you had been their agent instead.

When I bought my home, I had to go through a lot of red tape and running around, or at least it seemed that way you me. I worked with a buyer broker, which is common in my area. I live in a very competitive market, and I bought in September—a peak season. My broker was often unreachable, not calling me back for days, which was very frustrating. I discovered the property myself, at an open house. I remembered how helpful and detail oriented the seller's agent was, and when it came time for my sister to buy a place, I recommended the seller's broker. My sister had a wonderful experience with her broker. In fact, he was always calling her to check in throughout the closing process, which took much longer than expected. My sister and I have both recommended this broker to friends.

—TED CHARLES, a new home owner from New York City

WAYS OF KEEPING IN TOUCH

What are some methods of keeping in touch with former clients? Ideally, you want something that's inexpensive to produce but seems thoughtful. Different types of communication have different strengths and weaknesses. A few choices:

✓ **Letters**—Laser-printed letters are both professional and inexpensive but can be impersonal. Hand-printed letters are impractical in quantity. Letters are useful if you're trying to convey more than a few tidbits of information, such as the groundbreaking of a new development, or if you have something important to pass on to your clients, such as changing agency affiliation.

✓ **Cards**—Cards are more expensive than letters but also seem more personal, especially if you can add a few words in addition to your signature. Cards may be sent out in bulk or on special occasions for your clients, such as the anniversary of when they bought their houses. (This requires a ferocious level of organization).

✓ **Calendars**—The most expensive option is to send out calendars to clients every year, but if your calendars are nice, clients will be looking at your name and logo literally every day of the year. (There's no point in sending out a cheap-looking or ugly calendar, as it will only be thrown out.) Be careful about sending out calendars. They're a big investment, and if you're in an area where clients receive several calendars from other companies, your money can easily be wasted.

✓ **E-mail**—This is the cheapest way to stay in contact, but it's not very memorable or long lasting. Use e-mail if you want to send out a monthly newsletter, for example, but don't want your clients to be bothered by a bulk mailing four times a year. E-mail is also fine for informal reminders, and you can send cards via e-mail, as well.

WHEN TO FOLLOW UP

You want your former clients to hear from you regularly, but you don't want the message to be lost. You may want to think twice about sending cards at the same time when everyone else is sending holiday cards. (On the other hand, many real estate agents like to send holiday cards since people see their families at the holidays, and it's a good time for referrals.) Try Thanksgiving or New Year's to set your card apart from the typical holiday rush.

Here are some ideas for when to send cards or other follow up material to clients. Anytime you send cards or letters, enclose a few business cards, so people can give them out to interested friends and relatives. If you send more than one mailing a year, you may want to send use an online card service, such as bluemountain.com, or the card service at amazon.com. People will be happy to hear from you but don't want to feel like they're getting constant mailings from you.

SUMMING UP

Don't assume that buyers who are happy with the job you did will automatically refer you to their family and friends. You have to be willing to ask for referrals.

Make sure to stay in touch with your former clients. Try to contact them about once a year in a way that encourages them to think positively of you and refer others to you.

THE INTERNET AND REAL ESTATE

+ HOW TO USE THE INTERNET AS A TOOL TO BOOST YOUR SALES

+ HOW TO AVOID LOSING SALES TO INTERNET REAL ESTATE FIRMS

The Internet has been both a friend and an enemy to real estate agents. The Web provides you with sales tools and access to helpful information. It allows agencies to support their agents on a national as well as a local level. But it also leads to some very confused clients and predatory real estate sites that may try to take your clients. And there are many real estate and banking scams on the Web. Like many new technologies, the Internet is changing the way real estate works in some important ways, but in other ways you'll want to be skeptical of some of the Web's as-yet unfulfilled promises.

SELLING HOUSES ON THE INTERNET

It has become more and more common to list houses on the Internet. Houses are posted on major real estate sites like www.realtor.com, on agency sites, on individual agents' Web pages, on private commercial real estate sites, or some combination of these. The theory is that someone hunting for a house can specify the general area of the house and the criteria (such as cost and size), and get a list of available houses, complete with pictures, pertinent details, and a contact e-mail address to reach the listing agent. The more sophisticated sites may allow potential buyers to take a virtual tour of the house, as well.

The Internet is a comparatively inexpensive way to advertise your listings. Agency sites are generally provided as part of your listing with an agency, and many real estate sites provide you with a Web page either for free or for a small fee. It pays to read the fine print, though, since commercial sites will take a cut of any commissions they refer to you.

Are many people buying houses over the Internet? Yes and no. More and more people are visiting real estate sites, attracted by promises of free information or the lure of looking at houses from their own homes. It's common for people to browse the Web until they identify a particular area that seems appealing and then contact an agent whose name they saw while browsing so they can begin to actually visit houses.

It's also typical to get inquiries from people who see houses on the Web but aren't seriously prepared to buy yet. Because the Internet allows people to browse houses without any screening or prior discussion with a real estate agent, real estate sites have an open house quality to them—with many visitors using them as part of the process of deciding whether to buy a house rather than shopping for a specific house. You may get many e-mail inquiries about houses you've listed that people have seen on the Web, but few of those people will follow up on your responses. Be certain you answer those e-mail queries quickly, however, since many of those undecided buyers will end up buying a house in the future—and they'll remember the real estate agent who was helpful to them while they were "just looking."

Virtual Tours

In theory, virtual tours allow buyers to explore properties they might be interested in from the comfort of their own homes. Most of the major real estate sites offer Internet-based tours. The quality and depth of these tours varies from site to site. Some only allow you to pan around the outside of a house, while others have interior views, as well.

Unless you have a very fast Internet connection and an up-to-date computer, most virtual tours are maddeningly slow—you often have to wait for new images to load with each movement. Many tours also require buyers to load special viewing software into their systems, which some people will be reluctant to do. There's another time factor, as well: In fast real estate markets, the houses already have sold by the time they've been posted to the website.

Still, virtual tours have a high-tech quality to them and can be a useful sales tool. If your clients want to show a house to a relative halfway across the country, they can do so via the Internet. Buyers with limited mobility or access to the area—such as a buyer who is eight months' pregnant, or working across the country—can use real estate sites and virtual tours to narrow their search, and then focus on the houses that looked most alluring on the Web in the limited amount of time they have to look at houses with you.

E-mail

As a real estate sales agent, you can't get by without an e-mail address these days, any more than you can get by without a cell phone or fax machine. Clients won't keep the same hours you do and won't always want to call you with information. Buyers who want to ask you a question at midnight are likely to send it by e-mail, rather than waiting until morning to call you. Clients will expect to see an e-mail address on your cards; even if they never use it to contact you, it tells them that you're abreast of changing technologies.

You may get an e-mail address through the agency where you work. If not, you can get Internet service (usually including e-mail, Web access, and a Web page) through a national service such as America Online (AOL) or through a local Internet service provider (ISP). Check with other agents or friends to find out which ISPs in your area provide the best and most reliable service. (Most Sunday newspapers have a section of ISP ads.) Expect to pay $20 to $30 a month for Internet access.

Make sure you check your e-mail regularly. Try to check at least four times a day, including first thing in the morning and before you go to bed at night.

WEB PAGES

In today's digital economy, a website isn't really just an option any more—you have to have one. You may be provided with Web space through your agency or your Internet service provider. Unless you already know how to create a website, you will have to hire someone to create it for you. (It's not that hard to create a basic website, but you need to spend your first months as a real estate agent out finding clients, not sitting at home learning how to write in HTML.)

Typically, an inexpensive website can be created for several hundred dollars. Chances are, you've got a friend or family member who will be willing to create the site for a nominal cost to help you as you get started. You will provide the content (meaning the text and pictures) to whoever is creating the site.

Things you want to put on your website include:

✓ **Your picture**—A professional portrait is a good idea. This is the image most people will first see of you.

✓ **Contact information**—Address, phone, fax, and e-mail address. (Putting your e-mail address on the Web will expose you to a certain amount of unsolicited junk e-mail, but that's a necessary evil.)

✓ **Information about yourself and your agency**—What do you want clients to know about you? What image do you want them to have of you when they see your website?

✓ **What areas you work in**—Are there particular kinds of properties you prefer to sell? What geographic areas or neighborhoods do you do most of your business in?

✓ **Pictures of some properties**—Show a few properties that you've sold, or that you'd like to sell, to give people an idea of the kinds of properties you most like to show.

✓ **Links to other real estate–related sites**—This gives people an easy way to take virtual tours of houses in your area.

✓ **Links to mortgage sites**—Many mortgage sites have interest rate information, mortgage calculators, and other helpful information for buyers.

You want your site to stand out, but avoid overdoing it. Some things to watch out for:

✓ Make certain your text is easy to read. It shouldn't have any garish colors or blend into the background.

✓ Proofread the text for typos.

✓ Too many graphics will make your site load very slowly (if customers are using a dial-up modem). Make sure your site will load quickly even for people with older computers or slower modems. Also, make certain it can be read by different browsers (software that allows people to use the Internet), such as Microsoft Internet Explorer and Netscape Navigator.

✓ Websites that play music can be annoying to clients when the music repeats over and over.

DOMAIN NAMES

You may want to have a catchy name for your site or a website with your name on it. A "domain name," as website names are called, is not particularly expensive. You can register any name that hasn't already been taken for $35 a year (with a two-year commitment up front). To find out if the name you want to use is taken, go to www.networksolutions.com or www.register.com, and type in the name you're interested in. The site will tell you who owns the name, or if it's available for purchase (which can also be done online).

SECURITY ISSUES

There's an old cliché that you shouldn't put anything on the Internet that you wouldn't want to read on the front page of *The New York Times*. That may be an exaggeration, but do not take Internet security for granted. Anything posted on a website is open to the public, and even information posted to private areas may be found out easily by other people. Some things to be careful of:

✓   At least one real estate site posted lockbox and security system combinations for houses that were being shown. If you provide that information on a website and one of your client's houses is broken into as a result, you are potentially liable. You may want to avoid mentioning lockboxes at all, since the vast majority of lockboxes are never changed from their factory preset combinations, and those combinations are widely known among burglars. If you are the listing agent, just make sure there's enough contact information on the site so that if potential buyers or other agents want to look at the house, they can call you to set it up.

✓   Be careful what pictures you use on virtual tours. Anyone can look at these tours—and a series of pictures that depict the locations of a home's valuables, along with specific information about the layout of the home and where to find it, may be an invitation to theft.

✓   Don't take it for granted that your e-mail or your clients' is private. Discourage clients from e-mailing you personal or financial information from their work e-mail accounts unless their employer allows it. Many employers restrict e-mail usage or monitor employees' e-mail.

WEB TOOLS FOR REAL ESTATE AGENTS

This section of the book is an annotated selection of real estate–related websites. The list includes tools for agents, buyers, and sellers, as well as some sites that directly compete with you for business. You may want to spend some time browsing the sites in this chapter to see which ones will be helpful to you in particular areas and to gain an idea of some of the tools that you have available to you.

At the time of publication, the websites listed here were current. Due to the ever-changing nature of the Web, we cannot guarantee their continued existence or content.

NATIONWIDE AGENCY SITES

These sites are designed to connect buyers and sellers to a particular agency. Most have links to all of the company's agencies or franchisees nationwide. Typically, they also have advice for buyers and sellers and other tools to make the site (and the agency) attractive to the buyer, such as home valuation calculators or national neighborhood comparisons. All have mortgage links. Some sites have tools for agents to use, as well.

CENTURY 21

www.century21.com

A wide-ranging site that contains resources for buyers, sellers, and owners and access to training and support materials for Century 21 agents.

COLDWELL BANKER

www.coldwellbanker.com

Mainly material for buyers and sellers, including mortgage information.

RE/MAX

www.remax.com

Contains news articles for buyers, sellers, and owners, exchange rate and
mortgage information, as well as tools and training for RE/MAX
agents.

REAL ESTATE SITES

These sites are not connected with major agencies but have links to properties and agents nationwide.

HOMEADVISOR

www.homeadvisor.msn.com

Provides information on buying, selling, financing, or improving a
home. Also helps you move or relocate and redecorate your home.

HOMESEEKERS.COM

www.homeseekers.com

Designed to help buyers and sellers get information on houses and connect with real estate agents.

There are also many regional sites for home buyers, such as HAR.com
in the Houston area and buyersnetwork.com in New England.

Mortgage Sites

Mortgage sites generally include information, loan rates, and application forms for potential buyers to apply online. Some sites are designed for agents to help place hard-to-finance buyers. A few of the major mortgage sites include:

AMERICA MORTGAGE ONLINE
www.amo-mortgage.com
Includes mortgage tools, articles, extensive resources, and a search engine.

E-LOAN
www.eloan.com
Provides mortgages, refinancing, and credit information, along with calculators and a mortgage glossary.

FEDERAL HOUSING AUTHORITY (FHA)
www.fhatoday.com
Includes FHA information, downloadable loan documentation, and an online application for FHA loans.

LION, INC.
www.lioninc.com
Designed to help agents find lenders for buyers, especially for subprime or difficult-to-place loans.

MORTGAGE IT!
www.mortgageit.com
Includes a lot of information about mortgaging a home and offers online mortgaging. It also has an interactive datebase and a one-hour callback service for applicants.

THE MORTGAGE SOURCE ONLINE
www.mortgage-source.com

Designed to help buyers gather information and find an appropriate lender. A good source for national, regional, or local mortgage information.

FSBO Sites

These sites cater to owners selling their own homes. Many have only a few homes listed in each area. The biggest sites offer virtual tours, but the quality is generally well below that of the professional real estate sites. These sites may be a useful source of new clients (see page 38) or a cautionary lesson to potential sellers asking why they should hire you rather than sell their home themselves: Many of the properties have been listed for months or even years.

www.buyowner.com
www.byownersales.com
www.by-owner-ol.com
www.fisbos.com
www.fsbo.com
www.fsboadvertisingservice.com
www.fsbonetwork.com
www.fsbo-home.com
www.mls-fsbo.com
www.owners.com
www.propertyclassifiedsy2k.com

Online Resources for Real Estate Agents

These sites cater particularly to real estate agents, providing services and information that should be helpful to you. Some of these sites are free and some require subscription or other payment for services.

AMERICAN REAL ESTATE SOCIETY (ARES)
www.aresnet.org
A society of real estate professionals and professors.

THE AMERICAN REAL ESTATE AND URBAN ECONOMICS
ASSOCIATION
www.areuea.org
A nonprofit group devoted to real estate development, planning, and
economics.

BUILDFIND NETWORK
www.buildfind.com
A portal site for real estate and building industry web resources and
channels.

CENTER FOR REAL ESTATE STUDIES (CRES)
www.indiana.edu/~cres/welcome.htm
Real estate research and educational material hosted by the Indiana
University School of Business.

COMMERCIAL REAL ESTATE AND APPRAISAL WEB SITES
http://www1.shore.net/~straub/comweb.htm
A vast portal to many other real estate and appraisal websites.

COUNSELORS OF REAL ESTATE (CRE)
www.cre.org
A group of real estate professionals who provide advisory services on
complex property and land-related matters.

FIRST AMERICAN REAL ESTATE SOLUTIONS
www.firstamres.com
Provides real estate and mortgage finance data.

GLOBE STREET
www.globest.com
Real estate news site, with an articles archive, and a mailing list.

GUIDE TO RESOURCES ON REAL ESTATE
http://libraries.mit.edu/rotch/realestate/rehomepage.html
A guide to resources available online or in libraries, hosted by the
Massachusetts Institute of Technology.

INMAN REAL ESTATE NEWS
www.inman.com
A source for news on real estate–related issues.

INSTITUTE OF REAL ESTATE MANAGEMENT
www.irem.org
Business-to-business services and articles for real estate professionals.

INTERNET REALTY NETWORK
www.gorealty.com
Includes a variety of links, services, and other real estate resources.

INTERNATIONAL REAL ESTATE DIGEST
www.ired.com
Includes articles, information, and a directory of links in the real estate
industry.

ISUCCEED.COM
www.isucceed.com
Provides online continuing education, training, coaching, and information for agents and commercial services.

JACK BRAUSE LIBRARY
www.nyu.edu/library/rei
A part of New York University's Real Estate Institute, this site includes
an extensive selection of news (with an index of articles), discussion
groups, and links.

JOURNAL OF REAL ESTATE RESEARCH
http://business.fullerton.edu/journal
Scholarly real estate research published by the American Real Estate
Society (ARES).

NATIONAL ASSOCIATION OF CORPORATE REAL ESTATE
EXECUTIVES (NACORE)
www.nacore.com
Professional real estate managers organization; NACORE members
manage, buy, and sell real estate for corporations.

NEW YORK REAL ESTATE INSTITUTE
www.nyrei.com
Offers education programs for those who want to start a career in real
estate and real estate professionals who want to continue their education.

NORTH AMERICAN REAL ESTATE REVIEW
www.narer.com
A moderated real estate conference that allows registrants to discuss
issues that influence the development, financing, ownership, management, and use of property in America.

PIKENET
www.pikenet.com
A real estate marketplace, including news, job listings, tools, and other
free and pay services.

REAL ESTATE.COM
www.realestate.com
A commercial site providing software and Web solutions for real estate
agents, it includes free links as well as real estate tools (such as websites
and software geared to agents) for sale.

REAL ESTATE CYBERSPACE SOCIETY
www.recyber.com
An online service that helps real estate agent get onto the Web. Includes both free and pay services.

REAL ESTATE RESEARCH INSTITUTE
www.reri.org
Consists of scholarly research on real estate issues.

REALTOR.COM
www.realtor.com
The official site of the National Association of REALTORs, the site includes extensive resources for buyers and sellers as well as tools for agents. For more resources for REALTORs, see www.realtor.com/for-realtors and www.iMarketing. REALTOR.com, the subscription-based site for members.

REALTY TIMES
www.realtytimes.com
Includes real estate news and advice.

U.S. CENSUS BUREAU CONSTRUCTION STATISTICS
www.census.gov/ftp/pub/const/www/index.html
A source for information on home sales, housing starts, and other statistical material.

SUMMING UP

The Internet offers many attractive tools to buyers, sellers, and real estate agents, but not all of them work as advertised.

Virtual tours and other online tools can be used to attract buyers and showcase your listings, but few inquiries will turn into serious buyers.

Be careful of security issues on the Web. Avoid posting anything confidential on the Web or via e-mail.

It's important that you have your own e-mail address and website to remain competitive.

SPECIALIZED CASES, UNUSUAL SITUATIONS ... AND A LAST WORD

- WHAT DO YOU DO WHEN THINGS GO WRONG?
- HOW DO YOU HANDLE SOME OF THE LESS TYPICAL SITUATIONS THAT COME UP IN REAL ESTATE?

WHEN THINGS GO WRONG

Sometimes things don't go smoothly. People ask unanticipated questions, or negotiate irrationally, or make demands oblivious to their effects on the people around them. Here are some troubleshooting tips for dealing with problem situations that you may encounter during the process of helping people to buy and sell real estate.

TROUBLESOME QUESTIONS

How do you answer the questions you wish your clients hadn't asked? Sometimes clients ask you a question about a house that you are utterly unprepared for or completely didn't anticipate. Most of the time it's a bad idea to try to bluff your way out, especially if the clients know more about the topic than you do. On the other hand, you don't want to appear ignorant, especially if you feel the question is one you should know the answer to. And you don't want to sound like you're trying to avoid the question. Your best bet is to acknowledge the question and promise to follow up. So if a client asks, "Is this house part of the Heritage Corridor?" don't say "What Heritage Corridor?" Say "I'm not sure, but it may be. I'll have to find out which houses are part of it." Make a note of the question and make sure you actually do follow up. Clients will respect that you keep your word and care enough to gather extra information that's important to them.

Impossible Negotiators

Sometimes you run across people who are not negotiating for the same purpose that you are. They may want to buy or sell the property at hand, but sometimes that sale is secondary to something else in the negotiation. Unless you can address whatever it is that makes the person you are negotiating with adopt a particular style, the sale may fall through. Here are some types of negotiators and pointers on how to deal with them:

✓ **Win at all costs**—Some negotiators can't stomach anything less than total victory and seldom will give on even minor points. In order to get any concessions at all, you must ask for much more than you want and be prepared to give in on most of it, allowing the other parties to feel they have scored a major win by forcing you to give up so much.

✓ **Stubborn**—Sometimes people will fixate on a particular point and refuse to budge, no matter how trivial the point may seem or how impossible it is to grant. If the two parties can't find a solution or a way around the sticking point, it may be up to the agents. You may have to remind the other agent that his or her client is jeopardizing a $200,000 sale (and a sizable commission for the agent) over a $500 legal fee or over a zoning regulation that your clients don't have any power to change.

✓ **Ultracompetitive**—Some people love the give-and-take of the negotiating process and treat it as a sport or a competitive event that they
must win, instead of a process that both sides can work together on.
Encourage your client not to get involved in the competitive process,
and make sure all offers and counteroffers are in small increments, so
that the competitor can enjoy the thrill of wringing every last concession out of you. Make sure the competitor gives something back
or gives in on a condition for every concession or lowering in price
your client makes. Be prepared for a long process, but as long as the
negotiator's competitive spirit is satisfied, eventually the deal should
go smoothly.

✓ **Browbeaters**—Some people want to win by intimidating or
browbeating whomever they are negotiating with. Do not give in
to intimidation. If the person you are negotiating with makes
threats, don't be afraid to come right back with threats of your
own. A browbeater will take any ground you give as a sign of
weakness and will increase the level of the attack, probing for further weaknesses until you either stop giving in or collapse completely. You can make agreements with browbeaters, but you need
to be very firm in areas where you are in a good negotiating position and make concessions only where you are weakest. Once a
browbeater senses you will not give ground in a certain area, he or
she can be quite reasonable. You may be happy with the eventual
deal if you're not afraid to hold your ground and fight fire with fire,
but it's not a pleasant negotiating process.

✓ **Tough negotiators**—Some people are genuinely good negotiators, able to hone in on the weaknesses of your position and causing you to forget or underestimate your strengths. If you feel out-
classed, try to work away from the other negotiator's strengths. If
the person is a great talker and can smoothly convince you of any
position, then correspond by fax or e-mail. If you think you're
being outmaneuvered, never agree to anything on the spot; always
insist you have to go back and check something or get someone's

approval before finalizing anything. Don't be afraid to raise points again if you're not happy with how they were dealt with and no final agreement has been reached. Take your time, don't get flustered or give into pressure, and make sure the deal is fair and appropriate for your clients before agreeing to anything—even if the clients have given you prior approval to make the deal.

You want to try very hard to keep your clients from falling into negotiating traps. While being a difficult negotiator or needlessly confrontational may massage someone's ego, it makes real estate sales more difficult and time consuming, and seldom leads to a better deal than would be reached if all parties worked together in good faith.

LEVERAGE

Sometimes your clients have a lot of leverage, and sometimes they have very little. Make sure your clients are aware if their negotiating position is poor, and prepare them for tough negotiations. But there's no reason to let the other party know. Don't assume that the other party is working with the same set of assumptions you are or that their agent will correctly read your strengths and weaknesses—or their own. While you want to be realistic, you don't want to give away money, either.

✓ If you represent the seller and your client is under pressure to sell, resist the temptation to make concessions too soon. If you have to ask potential buyers to make an offer quickly, don't imply that your clients are desperate—give another reason, for instance, that the sellers will be hard to reach after the following week, so they wanted to move quickly. If an offer is made, your clients' counteroffer or acceptance can be conditional on the closing happening quickly, but at that point if the buyers' agent is savvy, he or she will probably realize that your clients are under pressure.

✓ If the house is in a very slow market or has been on the market for a long time, buyers are unlikely to offer full value. If the house has been on the market for as long as it has because the owners are under no pressure to sell, you may want to make the buyers aware of that, to help restore a little bit of leverage. They may make a higher offer if they know the sellers are not desperate to accept any offer, even though the market may be poor.

✓ If you represent buyers who have few options, see if you can create other possibilities for them, or at least give the sellers reason to believe they have other opportunities. If the buyers are locked into an FHA mortgage and the property is the only one eligible for an FHA mortgage that fits their criteria, you want to at least give the impression that your clients are willing to walk away if the sellers are unreasonable—while at the same time making it clear that your clients want to make a deal that's fair for all parties. Sometimes you can use weakness as a negotiating strength: "My clients would love to spend that, and it's certainly a fair price, but they just don't think they can afford to take on that much mortgage and still have the money to maintain the house."

WALKING AWAY

Sometimes negotiations break down, and buyers walk away from a deal. If you represent the sellers and you feel that the gap isn't unbridgeable, you may want to make one last effort—particularly if the property is a difficult one to sell or the market is weak in the area. Is there a concession the sellers can make that you can use to bring the buyers back? If there is, you can approach them. Be sure to move quickly, before the buyers have gotten over their desire for the house or have convinced themselves that they like their second choice better.

Don't act as if you are giving up something you could have given all along, or the buyers will feel manipulated and probably will not agree to return to the deal. Your approach should stress common ground and how close the deal was: "My clients have talked it over and they went over their finances again. As you know, they really wanted you to have the house, because your kids remind them of their own children when they were the same age. Anyway, they decided that if all that was standing in the way was that last $1,000, they could afford to make the deal."

Sometimes you may want to walk away as a strategy, but it is very risky. If there is a concession that your clients feel very strongly about, and you feel the sellers can give in on the point if they choose, and there are no other likely buyers present, you may want to let the sellers know that the point is a deal breaker, and your clients will walk away if the sellers can't give in on that one point. Be prepared to have your bluff called, however; there is usually only a 50-50 chance that the sellers will agree.

If the buyers and the sellers absolutely can't agree on a deal and the point is not a huge one, sometimes you and the other agent will be able to work together to find a solution, rather than have both of you lose the sale. Don't forget that the other agent is not your enemy; he or she wants the same thing you do—a successful sale—and neither of you should be burdened by the emotional ties to the property that the buyers and the sellers may have. Also remember that a successful sale is more important than being right or soothing your ego—you may have to ask your clients to give in on a point that you had counseled them not to, if it results in a deal that is fair to both sides. It's better to have you be a little embarrassed at having misjudged the other party than having everyone upset by a sale that has collapsed.

RECOVERING A LOST DEAL

One closing, there was a great deal of hostility between a seller I represented and the buyer. The buyers had been through the house a lot, and talked about how they were going to totally gut the house. The seller, who was older, resented that, even though he was getting asking price. He started screaming at the buyer over a $700 issue, and he said, "This closing is adjourned." The other agent and I got up and we walked out of the room to try to salvage the deal. We agreed to each cut our commission by $350 each and offer to make up the $700. We came back in and we said "We will pay for this" and then the closing went on.

—GAYLE DINERSTEIN

SAFETY

Pay attention to your own safety and that of your clients. Especially as a new agent, be careful about putting yourself into dangerous situations, and use common sense about where you take clients and when. While it's very rare, people have used the pretense of buying houses to assault real estate agents, and agents have been victimized while in unfamiliar neighborhoods at the wrong time.

✓ Always have a cell phone with a charged battery handy.

✓ Don't take clients into a neighborhood you're not comfortable in, especially not at night.

✓ Let someone know where you're traveling. Make sure there's a copy of your itinerary in your office and that someone knows where to find it. Include contact numbers for who you're seeing, where you're meeting them, what properties you're showing, and the times you expect to see them. Make sure your coworkers know what kind of car you drive, as well.

✓ If there's something about a client that makes you really uncomfortable, don't ignore it just because you really want to make the sale. Pay attention to warning signs.

✓ If a client says things that make you uncomfortable, cut the trip short. Invent an emergency if need be. Do not confront a harassing or belligerent client alone and away from any assistance. If it's just a misunderstanding, it can be cleared up in your office over coffee, not in a tense and potentially unsafe situation.

✓   If something looks strange about the house you're planning to see—for instance, if the door is ajar or you see someone wandering around in a house that's supposed to be empty—don't go in. Get a safe distance away and call the police. You don't want to walk in on a burglary.

COMPLEX SITUATIONS

It's not unusual for new real estate sales agents to find themselves in new and unfamiliar situations. While you've been trained for many of these situations, some of them will be hard to handle without experience. It's important not to let yourself get in over your head. There will be times when you will need to get a more experienced agent involved, rather than shortchange yourself and your clients. Be careful not to be so drawn in by the allure of a larger commission that you try to take on something you can't handle—and lose the entire commission, possibly wasting a client's time and money, as well.

Many real estate agents recommend finding a mentor—another agent you can work with, learn from, and turn to for advice during your first few months on the job. Doing so helps eliminate agents trying to take on big projects without support. As broker Ed Farthing puts it, "If you don't know what you're doing, you shouldn't be doing it. If you're not qualified to handle an apartment building, then don't list it. Rather than give up the business, you colist it with somebody. You go to an experienced agent in your office and say, 'Let's colist it.'" Some agencies have mentor programs for new agents while others do not; even if your agency does not, you should be able to find a more experienced agent who will be happy to help show you the ropes in return for helping him or her out (e. g., running open houses, as mentioned earlier).

This chapter discusses a few unusual situations you may encounter. Others, such as multifamily dwellings or land sales, vary so much from state to state and even town to town that you really do need to draw on a more experienced agent's help to handle them. Don't be afraid to ask for help where you need it; it's better to be embarrassed by asking questions or having someone look over paperwork than to have a sale blow up in your face— or worse, find yourself in legal or ethical trouble—due to inexperience.

INEXPERIENCE AND MENTORS

We had an experience with a two-family dwelling. A new agent sold it, and both sides were rented. The agent told the buyer that she would be taking possession the day of closing, when in fact she had to buy the property and then give thirty or sixty days' notice to the tenants. She had a very angry buyer, and it cost the buyer a lot of extra money. If she'd had a mentor, it's likely that this wouldn't have happened. Agents can't be expected to know everything the first time out. They are, however, expected to ask for help when necessary in order to act in their customer's best interest.

—PAT FARTHING

FORECLOSURES

Sometimes you'll find yourself selling a property where the owner is a bank or institution instead of a person. While you won't have to worry about any of the problems caused by temperamental or uncooperative sellers, foreclosure properties vary widely in condition. If the previous owners were responsible and careful owners, they probably would not have lost the house in the first place.

Frequently, lenders who are saddled with foreclosure properties do not adequately care for them. Be sure to look closely at a foreclosure property before you agree to represent it—and spend the money advertising it. Be certain the house actually is in salable condition.

✓ Just because the bank tells you the house is in good shape, don't assume that it is, or you may be surprised the first time you try to show the property. The bank's report is probably based on the condition the house was in when the bank took possession, and no one may have looked at it since that time. It's possible that no maintenance work has been done on the house at all. Before you show the house, go through and check for unsafe conditions and clean up any unsightly problems, such as dead birds that flew down the chimneys and got trapped.

✓ Insist that the house be kept in salable condition. Don't represent a house if the bank will not commit to at least routine maintenance. It's also important that the electricity be left on in the house, especially if an electric sump pump is the only thing that keeps the basement from flooding. If there's a pool, make sure it's covered securely and winterized, and there's a fence in place to keep the neighborhood kids away.

PART-TIME AGENTS

It's difficult to be a part-time agent, although many agents are. It's particularly hard if you're just starting out. Even if you eventually plan to cut back to part-time hours, it's best to sell full time until you've built up a network of contacts and referrals. As a part-time agent, you may not be available to visit open houses or to look at houses at a convenient time for your clients, so you'll have to make up for it with exemplary service and excellent people skills.

Some ways to make part-time agenting work:

✓ If you're available two days a week and on weekends, you should be able to meet most of your clients' needs. Build a partnership with someone in the office to make sure your clients are covered if you're not available.

✓   If you work another job when you're not selling real estate, be careful to avoid conflicts. Don't tie up your employer's phones with real estate business or spend your workday working on real estate instead of what your employer is paying you for.

✓   If you're switching gears between jobs frequently, it's even more important to stay organized. It will be very easy for material to be forgotten or fall through the cracks.

✓   You'll need to make an extraordinary effort to get to know the housing stock. Because you're not spending every day driving around the area and immersed in real estate, you will have to study what houses have become available.

RENTALS

Many real estate agents prefer not to handle rentals. The payoff—often one month's rent—isn't always very much considering the knowledge of local conditions and landlord-tenant law that you'll need. In certain areas, particularly urban locations, specialized agents handle many rentals.

Chances are that you will have to handle an occasional rental. Sometimes a good client who bought a property from you will later ask you to arrange a rental on a property as a favor. In some locations, such as seasonal resort areas, the market is heavily rental driven and it's very difficult for an agent who does not handle rentals to compete for listings.

Some things to keep in mind when handling rentals:

✓   In seasonal resorts, time is everything. If a house is rented by the week during the summer, you can't afford to lose a day having the house cleaned between the time one tenant leaves and the next arrives. Specialized cleaning crews are available that bring in many workers to clean a house in an hour or two. Find a crew that's reliable and unflappable.

✓   Some areas require you to obtain certificates of occupancy for
    rentals of houses or have other specific town requirements for
    renting property. Make sure you know and follow the local rental
    procedures. If there's a landlord-tenant problem later, you don't
    want to be fined by the town for an illegal rental (or have the
    owner of the property fined), especially if you were just doing
    someone a favor.

✓   Make sure the property is adequately insured. The owner's liabili-
    ty insurance may need to be revised or have a rider added to cover
    tenants. If tenants are staying in the property long term, you
    should encourage them to obtain renter's insurance.

✓   Take pictures of the property's interior and exterior between ten-
    ants. If there's any damage claim, you'll have a much better chance
    of staying out of landlord-tenant court if you have evidence to back
    your case.

✓   One way to avoid serious problem tenants is to check with the
    landlord-tenant court to make sure a potential tenant hasn't been
    involved in previous litigation. Often there's a computer kiosk or
    other easy way to check this information. You don't want to find
    yourself in court with a nuisance tenant when 15 minutes of
    checking would have unearthed eight previous lawsuits against the
    tenant's former landlords.

✓   Don't cut corners on security deposits. Most state laws require
    security deposits to be placed in escrow in an interest-bearing
    account. Tenants need to be sent regular statements, and there
    may be other paperwork requirements. Know the state laws and
    regulations regarding landlords and tenants. Most states have free
    publications and resources for landlords that will give you this
    information.

SUMMING UP

Sometimes you will run into negotiators who are belligerent or hard to deal with. If you stay calm and don't lose sight of your goals, you should still be able to complete a sale that is fair to your clients.

Don't forget about your own and your clients' safety when you're selling real estate.

If you're faced with a complex situation that is beyond your experience, get some help. It's easy to make major mistakes from inexperience.

If at all possible, find a mentor who can help you with advice and guidance during your first months as a real estate agent.

Make sure you learn any applicable state and local regulations if you're going to handle rentals or other functions that you haven't been specifically trained for.

THE LAST WORD

There's a lot of work in real estate, and you've already done a lot of work to get this far. But don't lose sight of the things that brought you into this profession—new challenges, independence, a fast-paced and exciting day, freedom from a drab office grind, and the possibility of an excellent income.

Real estate sales are something you have to work at very hard to be successful—but also something that you will enjoy along the way. You will always be meeting new and interesting people, and you will be making a positive difference in people's lives. The deals that you close will impact on your own life as much as the lives of your clients.

Work hard, but enjoy the work. Don't let the uncertainty of your first few months in real estate sales overshadow the brightness of your future.

WRITING ADS

Here are some dos and don'ts for creating advertisements for newspapers, flyers, and mailings.

PICTURES

✓ Always put a photo of yourself in your ads (or in the ads for your agency, if that's an option). No matter how much you hate to be photographed, it's important that people identify an image with you as you build a professional identity.

✓ Use a professional photo of yourself. This may be the first impression someone has of you, and you want to stand out (even if the quality of the ad reproduction is poor).

✓ Change photos occasionally, especially in agency ads. If the agency you work for runs a similar ad with photos in the masthead every week, people will get used to looking at it. They'll also notice if you've been running the same picture for the last five years.

✓ Use good photos of your listings. Nobody wants to look at blurry or muddy pictures of houses. If you're taking a lot of pictures for ads, you may want to invest in a digital camera, which will save you the cost of film and developing if you have to take a lot of pictures to get a few good ones. A cheap digital camera sells for less than $150, and you can get a good one for about $350 if you shop around. If you don't know anything about cameras, stick with name-brand digital cameras.

LANGUAGE

✓ Don't overuse quotation marks or exclamation points. They distract readers from the points you're trying to make and look amateurish.

✓ Check your spelling and grammar. Nobody trusts an agent who's too careless to double-check spelling.

✓ Use strong, active language. Vary your descriptive words so all your listings don't sound the same. For a list of powerful descriptive words, see Appendix B.

✓ Don't use too many long words. In a short ad, text has to flow quickly. Because most readers will only look at it for a second or two, you want your writing to jump off the page and be quickly understandable.

✓ Don't use words unless you're sure of what they mean. If you're not sure, look the word up before you embarrass yourself.

✓ Don't overdescribe. It's better to use one perfect word instead of piling on adjectives that bog down your ad copy.

✓   Avoid abbreviations. If an ad has too many abbreviations, it can be very hard to read. Stick to abbreviations that are easy to understand—remember that most of the people looking at your ad are first-time home buyers, not seasoned real estate professionals who are familiar with all the terms.

✓   Avoid jargon and buzz words.

✓   Don't say something is "more" or "better" unless you say what something is more than. Also, never say "more unique." Unique means *one of a kind*, so a property either is unique or it isn't—it can't be more or less so.

POWER WORDS
AND PHRASES

Use these words for describing houses in your ads, flyers, letters, and conversations. Remember, it's better to use one perfect word than three or four not-quite-as-good ones. Avoid piling on meaningless modifiers like "more" or "totally"; find the exact word you want instead. Always be as specific as possible to make your listings stand out.

PROPERTY-SPECIFIC WORDS

airy
amenities
ample
antique
beachfront
beautiful

brand new
breathtaking
bright
bustling (neighborhood)
captivating
cathedral ceilings

central
charming
child-friendly
city view
classic
clean
colonial
comfortable
community
conveniences
cozy
craftsmanship
custom
delightful
desirable
distinguished
dramatic
easy
easy financing
elegant
excellent
exciting
exclusive
expansive
exquisite
extraordinary
features
federal
fine
garden
gem
glamorous
gorgeous
graceful
great location

handsome
hardwood floors
haven
high ceilings
historic
homey
ideal
immaculate
incomparable
incredible
lake view
large
lifestyle
lively
location
luxurious
magnificent
matchless
modern
new
open
opportunity
original
outstanding
panoramic view
parks
peaceful
perfect
preeminent
premier
prestigious
pristine
private
quaint
quality

quiet
rare
refuge
remarkable
remodeled
renovated
restored
rich
roomy
rustic
safe
scenic
secluded
security
serene
solid
sophisticated
southern exposure
spacious
special
spectacular
spotless
stable

storage
strong
stunning
sturdy
sunny
superior
terrific
ultimate
unique
unmatched
unparalleled
updated/up to date
upscale
value
vibrant
victorian
view
vista
waterfront
well kept
well maintained
workmanship

GENERAL DESCRIPTIVE WORDS

accomplish
accountability
achieve
advertising
advice
aggressive
analyze

attain
available
care
careful
client's best interests
client focused
concern

consideration
contacts
coordinated
creative
customer service and satisfaction
detail oriented
develop
driven
dynamic
effective
efficient
effort
established
expedite
facilitate
focus
goals
identify

improve
initiate
marketing
negotiate/negotiable
network
organized
plan
prepare
proactive
proven
punctual
reputation
respect
responsibility
service
track record
value
x-year history

RESOURCES

The following groups provide support or services you may find useful. This list includes real estate trade groups as well as related services, such as appraisers, home inspectors, and relocation services. At the time of publication, the websites listed here were current. Due to the dynamic nature of the Web, we cannot guarantee their continued existence or content. For additional online resources, see list beginning page 149.

ACCOLADE NETWORK, INC. (REAL ESTATE APPRAISER NETWORK)
National Assignment Center
415 G Street
Modesto, CA 95351
Phone: 209-522-9981
www.appraise.com

ALLISON APPRAISALS (NATIONWIDE APPRAISAL SERVICE)
Phone: 800-286-6635
www.aappraisals.com
e-mail: mail@allisonappraisals.com

AMERICAN INDUSTRIAL REAL ESTATE ASSOCIATION
700 S. Flower Street, Suite 600
Los Angeles, CA 90017
Phone: 213-687-8777
www.airea.com

AMERICAN INSTITUTE OF CERTIFIED PLANNERS
1776 Massachusetts Avenue N.W., Suite 400
Washington, DC 20036
Phone: 202-872-0611
www.planning.org

AMERICAN LAND TITLE ASSOCIATION
1828 L Street N.W., Suite 705
Washington, DC 20036
Phone: 202-296-3671
www.alta.org

AMERICAN PLANNING ASSOCIATION
122 S. Michigan Avenue, Suite 1600
Chicago, IL 60603-6107
Phone: 312-431-9100
www.planning.org

THE AMERICAN REAL ESTATE SOCIETY (ARES)
College of Business and Public Administration
Gamble Hall, Room 160A
University of North Dakota
P.O. Box 7120
Grand Forks, ND 58202-7120
Phone: 701-777-3670
www.aresnet.org

THE AMERICAN REAL ESTATE AND URBAN ECONOMICS ASSOCIATION
(AREUEA)
Indiana University, Kelley School of Business
1309 East Tenth Street, Suite 738
Bloomington, Indiana 47405
Phone: 812-855-7794
www.areuea.org
e-mail: AREUEA@indiana.edu

AMERICAN SOCIETY OF APPRAISERS
555 Herndon Parkway, Suite 125
Herndon, VA 20170
Phone: 703-478-2228
www.appraisers.org

AMERICAN SOCIETY OF ASSET MANAGERS
303 W. Cypress Street
P.O. Box 12528
San Antonio, TX 78212
Phone: 800-486-3676
e-mail: czh@lincoln-grad.org

AMERICAN SOCIETY OF FARM MANAGERS AND RURAL APPRAISERS
950 S. Cherry Street, Suite 508
Denver, CO 80246
Phone: 303-758-3513
www.asfmra.org

AMERICAN SOCIETY OF HOME INSPECTORS
932 Lee Street, Suite 101
Des Plaines IL 60016-6546
Phone: 800-743-ASHI
www.ashi.com

THE APPRAISAL FOUNDATION
1029 Vermont Avenue N.W., Suite 900
Washington, DC 20005-3517
Phone: 202-347-7722
www.appraisalfoundation.org

APPRAISAL INSTITUTE
875 N. Michigan Avenue, Suite 2400
Chicago, IL 60611-1980
Phone: 312-335-4100
www.appraisalinstitute.org

BUILDING OWNERS AND MANAGERS ASSOCIATION INTERNATIONAL
1201 New York Avenue N.W., Suite 300
Washington, DC 20005
Phone: 202-408-2662
www.boma.org

COMMERCIAL INVESTMENT REAL ESTATE INSTITUTE
430 N. Michigan Avenue, 8th Floor
Chicago, IL 60611-4092
Phone: 800-621-7027
www.ccim.com

COMMUNITY ASSOCIATIONS INSTITUTE
225 Reinekers Lane Suite 300
Alexandria, VA 22314
Phone: 703-548-8600
www.caionline.org

EMPLOYEE RELOCATION COUNCIL
1720 N Street N.W.
Washington, DC 20036
Phone: 202-857-0857
www.erc.org

ENVIRONMENTAL SYSTEMS RESEARCH INSTITUTE, INC. (GEOGRAPHIC
INFORMATION SYSTEM (GIS) AND MAPPING SERVICES)
380 New York Street
Redlands, CA 92373-8100
Phone: 800-447-9778
www.esri.com

HOME INSPECTIONS—USA
Home Inspection Directory Corp.
P.O. Box 1465
North Hampton, NH 03862
Phone: 877-491-2171
www.homeinspections-usa.com

HOTEL AND MOTEL BROKERS OF AMERICA
1420 N.W. Vivion, Suite 111
Kansas City, MO 64118
Phone: 800-821-5191
www.hmba.com

INMAN REAL ESTATE NEWS
1250 45th Street, Suite 360
Emeryville, CA 94608
Phone: 510-685-9317
www.inman.com
e-mail: info@inman.com

INSTITUTE OF REAL ESTATE MANAGEMENT
430 N. Michigan Avenue
Chicago, IL 60611-4090
Phone: 312-329-6000
www.irem.org

INTERNATIONAL ASSOCIATION OF ASSESSING OFFICERS
130 E. Randolph Street, Suite 850
Chicago, IL 60601
Phone: 312-819-6100
www.iaao.org

INTERNATIONAL REAL ESTATE INSTITUTE
1224 North Nokomis N.E.
Alexandria, MN 56308
Phone: 320-763-4648
www.iami.org/irei.cfm
e-mail: irei@iami.org

INTERNATIONAL RIGHT OF WAY ASSOCIATION
Pacifica Harbor Business Center, Suite 220
19750 S. Vermont Avenue
Torrance, CA 90502-1144
Phone: 310-538-0233
www.irwaonline.org

MANUFACTURED HOUSING INSTITUTE
2101 Wilson Boulevard., Suite 610
Arlington, VA 22201-3062
Phone: 703-558-0400
www.mfghome.org

MORTGAGE BANKERS ASSOCIATION OF AMERICA
1919 Pennsylvania Avenue, N.W.
Washington, DC 20006-3438
Phone: 202-557-2700
www.mbaa.org

NACORE INTERNATIONAL (FORMERLY INTERNATIONAL ASSOCIATION
OF CORPORATE REAL ESTATE EXECUTIVES)
440 Columbia Drive, Suite 100
West Palm Beach, FL 33409
Phone: 800-726-8111
www.nacore.com

NATIONAL APARTMENT ASSOCIATION, EDUCATIONAL DEPARTMENT
201 N. Union Street, Suite 200
Alexandria, VA 22314
Phone: 703-518-6141
www.naahq.org

NATIONAL ASSOCIATION OF HOME BUILDERS
1201 15th Street, N.W.
Washington, DC 20005
Phone: 202-822-0200
www.nahb.com

NATIONAL ASSOCIATION OF HOME INSPECTORS
4248 Park Glen Road
Minneapolis, MN 55416
Phone: 800-448-3942
www.nahi.org

NATIONAL ASSOCIATION OF INDEPENDENT FEE APPRAISERS
7501 Murdoch Avenue
St. Louis, MO 63119
Phone: 314-781-6688
www.naifa.com

NATIONAL ASSOCIATION OF MASTER APPRAISERS
303 W. Cypress Street
San Antonio, TX 78212-0617
Phone: 800-229-6262
www.masterappraisers.com

NATIONAL ASSOCIATION OF MORTGAGE BROKERS
8201 Greensboro Drive, Suite 300
McLean, VA 22102
Phone: 703-610-9009
www.namb.org

NATIONAL ASSOCIATION OF REAL ESTATE EDITORS (NAREE)
1003 N.W. 6th Terrace
Boca Raton, FL 33486
Phone: 561-391-3599
www.naree.org
e-mail: madkimba@aol.com

NATIONAL ASSOCIATION OF REAL ESTATE APPRAISERS
1224 North Nokomis N.E.
Alexandria, MN 56308
Phone: 320-763-7626
www.iami.org/narea.cfm
e-mail: narea@iami.org

NATIONAL ASSOCIATION OF REAL ESTATE BROKERS
1629 K Street N.W., Suite 1100
Washington, DC 20006
Phone: 202-785-4477
www.nareb.com
e-mail: info@nareb.com

NATIONAL ASSOCIATION OF REALTORS
700 11th Street, N.W.
Washington, DC 20001
Phone: 202-383-1000
www.realtor.com

NATIONAL ASSOCIATION OF RESIDENTIAL PROPERTY MANAGERS
P.O. Box 140647
Austin, TX 78714-0647
Phone: 800-782-3452
www.narpm.org
e-mail: info@narpm.org

NATIONAL PROPERTY MANAGEMENT ASSOCIATION
1108 Pinehurst Road, Oaktree Center
Dunedin, FL 34698
Phone: 727-736-3788
www.npna.org

NATIONAL PROPERTY VALUATION, INC.
7915 FM 1960 W., Suite 229
Houston, TX 77070-5716
Phone: 281-807-6363
www.npvusa.com
e-mail: npv@npvusa.com

NATIONAL RESIDENTIAL APPRAISERS INSTITUTE
2001 Cooper Foster Park Road
Amherst, OH 44001
Phone: 440-282-7925
www.nraiappraisers.com
e-mail: info@rfpi.com

REAL ESTATE BROKERAGE MANAGERS COUNCIL
430 N. Michigan Avenue
Chicago, IL 60611-4092
Phone: 800-621-8738
www.crb.com

REAL ESTATE EDUCATORS ASSOCIATION
320 West Sabal Palm Place, Suite 150
Longwood, FL 32779
Phone: 407-834-6688
www.reea.org

REAL ESTATE LAW INSTITUTE
303 W. Cypress Street
San Antonio, TX 78212
Phone: 210-225-2897

THE REAL ESTATE PROFESSIONAL MAGAZINE
Wellesley Publications, Inc.
Needham, MA 02492
Phone: 781-444-4688
www.therealestatepro.com

REALTORS® LAND INSTITUTE (FORMERLY FARM AND LAND INSTITUTE)
430 N. Michigan Avenue
Chicago, IL 60611
Phone: 800-441-LAND
www.rliland.com
e-mail: rli@realtors.org

REALTY TIMES
5949 Sherry Lane, Suite 1250
Dallas, TX 75225
Phone: 214-353-6980
www.realtytimes.com

SOCIETY OF INDUSTRIAL AND OFFICE REALTORS®
700 11th Street N.W., Suite 510
Washington, DC 20001-4511
Phone: 202-737-1150
www.sior.com

URBAN LAND INSTITUTE
1025 Thomas Jefferson Street, N.W., Suite 500 West
Washington, DC 20007-5201
Phone: 800-321-5011
www.uli.org

WOMEN'S COUNCIL OF REALTORS®
430 N. Michigan Avenue
Chicago, IL 60611
Phone: 312-329-8483
www.wcr.org

INDEX

farming neighborhoods, 61-62
first meeting with, 68-70
freebies, 59-60
getting buyers to make an offer, 95-96
getting preapproved, 75-78
getting to the offer, 94-106
listening to, 71-72, 90
local media, 62-63
meeting with couples, 72
negotiating points for, 78-79
new homes, 64
open houses, 60-61
organizations, 63
physical disabilities and, 72-73
prejudging clients, 54-55
preparing of, 66-67
referrals, 65-66
relocations, 64-65
repeat visits, 93-94
showing homes to, 88-89
sponsorships, 63-64
techniques for finding, 55-66
typical questions for, 68
buzz words, and things to avoid, 90

calendars, and following up, 141
car expenses, 11
cards and flyers, 55, 56-58, 62
    following up, 141
cars, and strengths, 18-19
cell phones, 12
Center for Real Estate Studies (CRES), 153
Century 21, 149
Charles, Ted, and keeping in touch, 141
childcare, 11
children, impact of, 47
chit chat, and wasting time, 21
clients, see buyers
closings, 130-135
    smooth closings, 133
    walk-throughs, 132-133
clothes, 10-11
cold-call techniques, 28-30
Coldwell Banker, 38, 150
Coldwell Banker George T. Decker, 38
colistings, 166
Commercial Investment Real Estate Institute, 185

Commercial Real Estate and Appraisal Web Sites, 153
community activities, and selling points, 85
Community Associations Institute, 185
complex situations, 166-170
conditional acceptance, 116
contingencies, 104, 111, 113
Counselors of Real Estate (CRE), 153
counteroffers, 116, 121-123

Dinerstein, Gayle
    finding a neighborhood, 34
    listening to buyers, 71-72
    prejudging clients, 54
    recovering a lost deal, 164-165
Dinerstein, Roberta, and preparing sellers, 47-48
diplomacy, 99-100, 134-135, 138
    preventing clashes, 123
domain names, and Internet, 148
downside for new agents, 10-14
dual agencies, 5, 67
    formulating offers, 103-105

E-Loan, 151
e-mail, 145-146
    following up, 141
eating out, entertaining clients, 12
emotional attachments, 42-43
Employee Relocation Council, 185
employment, and negotiating points, 118
energy audit, negotiating opportunities, 49
energy efficiency, and selling points, 84
energy level, 17-18, 21
entertaining clients, 12
environment, and selling points, 85
Environmental Systems Research Institute, Inc. (Geographic Information System (GIS) and Mapping Services), 185
estate sales, 37
exercise, 14
expectations, 22-23
    unrealistic expectations, 50
expired listings, 26, 36-37
explaining the offer to the sellers, 114-115

failing inspection, 129
failure, and why agents fail, 9-10